SOCIAL MEDIA AND PARTICIPATORY DEMOCRACY

This book is part of the Peter Lang Media and Communication list.
Every volume is peer reviewed and meets
the highest quality standards for content and production.

PETER LANG
New York • Bern • Frankfurt • Berlin
Brussels • Vienna • Oxford • Warsaw

SHANNON E. MARTIN

SOCIAL MEDIA AND PARTICIPATORY DEMOCRACY

Public Notice AND THE World Wide Web

PETER LANG
New York • Bern • Frankfurt • Berlin
Brussels • Vienna • Oxford • Warsaw

Library of Congress Cataloging-in-Publication Data

Martin, Shannon E., author.
Social media and participatory democracy: public notice
and the World Wide Web / Shannon E. Martin.
pages cm
Includes bibliographical references and index.
1. Government information—Law and legislation—United States.
2. Notice (Law)—United States
3. Social media—Law and legislation—United States.
4. Internet in public administration—United States. I. Title.
KF5753.M325 342.73'066—dc23 2014000546
ISBN 978-1-4331-2302-3 (hardcover)
ISBN 978-1-4331-2301-6 (paperback)
ISBN 978-1-4539-1317-8 (e-book)

Bibliographic information published by **Die Deutsche Nationalbibliothek**.
Die Deutsche Nationalbibliothek lists this publication in the "Deutsche Nationalbibliografie"; detailed bibliographic data are available on the Internet at http://dnb.d-nb.de/.

The paper in this book meets the guidelines for permanence and durability of the Committee on Production Guidelines for Book Longevity of the Council of Library Resources.

29 Broadway, 18th floor, New York, NY 10006
www.peterlang.com

Printed in the United States of America

TABLE OF CONTENTS

PREFACE

Representative democracies depend on informed constituents to guide and oversee the officers who make the day-to-day decisions of government work. Voters, in turn, rely on information provided to them from those public officeholders in order to understand what needs to be done and which resources are available to accomplish the work. It is, at its most elegant, a feedback loop that works only as well as all the individual parts allow. Strong communication networks are one element of this loop that can make or break the success of the structure.

These communication networks not only help keep constituents informed about working governments' activities but also allow voters to observe how well public officeholders are working on behalf of the electorate. Greek city-states required public reports, and there were opportunities for citizens to ask officials during public meetings to justify what was done during their terms in office. As governments have grown larger and serve larger populations, additional systems have been put in place to provide similar opportunities for reporting.

Modern representative democracies usually include an array of communication platforms, including speeches that may be broadcast over the air, handbills posted in public gathering places, advertisements and meeting reports in newspapers, bulletin boards on social networking sites, government-hosted webpages, and email listservs. Though the range of communication vehicles is now as wide as it has ever been, the contents of the government messages are usually quite specific and guided by statute. These legal structures for providing government information to the electorate often include freedom of access laws, open meetings laws, and public notice requirements.

Freedom of access, sometimes referred to as FOA, and open meetings, often called sunshine laws, are political inventions of the twentieth century. Public notice, however, has been part of representative democracies since the earliest iterations of their organization. These public notices are usually provided in the form of a document when something is about to be done or has recently been done by government. For about 200 years, these notices have often taken the form of legal notices placed as classified ads in newspapers.

The majority of the work in this book treats those instances where governments are required to provide public notice when something is about to be done, or when something that has just been done on behalf of the electorate needs to be widely publicized. Community budgets, calls for contracts or bidding, and new laws or changes in structure are often the subjects of public notice announcements, sometimes called legal notices, but these are not the only kinds of notice provided. The variations on content for public notice will be detailed more fully in chapters of this book concerning the history and definitions of legal notice.

The early chapters of this book will contextualize the theoretical frames for public notice and pose some questions that seem to be gaining traction among governments and legal scholars. In order to answer these questions, the work will present historical and legal underpinnings for the broader claim of a public requirement to be informed about government. The research presented here focuses primarily on published public records referred to throughout the book as "public notices."

The penultimate chapter will report the kinds of changes that public notice and published public records have undergone as governments around the world try to accommodate the digital formats for information and World Wide Web publishing. The final chapter of the book will summarize the observations made in the previous chapters, and the author will make recommendations for smoothing the transition from a paper-based world of records to an environment of speed, virtual portability, and—if poorly managed—disastrous miscommunication.

The author is keenly aware of the fear voiced by some policy watchers that government information on the web will fall prey to pranks and misuse. While it is possible—even likely—that the learning curve for avoiding information loss and misunderstanding will be steep, we can perhaps shorten the period of pain and mismanagement by looking carefully at the intent of public notice and the history of democratic evolution. This work aims to provide some of that recollection.

ACKNOWLEDGMENTS

This book is the product of many helpful people. I am grateful to the librarians and staff of the Clements Library at the University of Michigan for providing Reese Fellowship support, and to the librarians and staff at the University of Michigan and Indiana University law libraries for their help in pointing me in the direction of their wonderful resources. Librarians have long been among my favorite people, and these particular members of that community are exemplary.

I also thank Mary Savigar at Peter Lang Publishing for encouraging me to begin this research project and for guiding me through the acquisition process. David Copeland at Elon University, Charles Davis, now at the University of Georgia, and Kathleen Hansen at the University of Minnesota all wrote support letters so that I had a chance at the Clements Library fellowship. Thanks go to my research assistant, Rachelle Pavelko, for her thorough copyediting.

As always, I thank my patient husband, Edwin Martin, for his attention and kindness as I buried myself in this research and writing when I probably should have been attending to other aspects of our lives. Similarly, my sister and her husband, my children, their spouses, and my grandchildren generously released me from familial duties with grace and good cheer so that

I could work on this project. I also thank my parents, Mary and Robert Rossi, for initially bringing this topic to my attention when I began my doctoral program two decades ago and for enthusiastically reading my draft papers along the way.

My boundless gratitude, however, goes to the many original thinkers across dozens of decades and geographies noted too briefly in the pages that follow. My biggest thrills were handling the original letters and scanning the quill's flourishes as new knowledge was being born centuries ago. In this digital age it is easy to believe that all great ideas were born after 1993, but we all owe an almost unbearable debt to the brave intellects who came out of civilizations now barely recognized. I hope this book extends their legacies just a bit longer.

Shannon E. Martin

· 1 ·

POLITICAL COMMUNICATION THEORIES AND THE DEVELOPMENT OF PUBLIC NOTICE

The rationale for any one element of a political system depends on the interplay of that element with all other parts of the system. Public notice, the subject of this book, has such a long history within democracies and representative government that it seems almost redundant to have to explain or justify its character and use. Political theory helps us in this case not only to place public notice in a social construct but also to appreciate its contribution as an element of a political system and predict how the system would change if this one element were to change.

A good discussion of political theory was presented by William Bluhm in his classic text *Theories of the Political System.*[1] Bluhm made the distinction between public government involving public politics and business or church government involving private politics. For the present work we will assume that public government and public politics are the subjects being discussed. Working on that premise, the political theory elements for us, here, will include the social process involving cooperation among those with power, leading to decision making for the group.

The relationship between and interplay of these elements—social processes, cooperation, the bestowing of power, and group decision making—remains a complicated network for government constructs. The chapters presented here will focus on representative democracies that are either long established or currently emerging. Though this form of government is not perfect for all social environments, it will provide the context for the following chapters of this book. The author is grateful that much has been written about the benefits and detriments of a representative democracy. The founding fathers of the United States of America rigorously debated the principles and the details for years, and much of that conversation can be found in *The Federalist Papers*, for example.[2]

These debates and those of the several centuries that followed preclude the necessity of arguing the merits of this form of government here. Instead, our attention will be focused on the particulars of communication between government functionaries and constituents within a representative democracy, acknowledging the strengths and weaknesses of the fundamental structure.

Political and Communication Theory

The need for effective communication between government functionaries and constituents in a representative democracy is clear from that social model's earliest examples. The Greek city-states routinely posted official documents in public places reporting the activities of government.[3] All citizens were expected to be well informed about public events before casting a vote or even speaking publicly about decisions to be made, so it is no surprise that government documents were important to social life. An example of the reasons given for creating and keeping such documents is part of an argument made by a well-known orator, Aeschines. While speaking in a law court, he is reported to have said in 330 B.C.E., "A fine thing, my fellow Athenians, a fine thing is the preservation of public records. For records do not change, and they do not shift sides with traitors, but they grant to you, the people, the opportunity to know whenever you want, which men, once bad, through some transformation now claim to be good."[4]

For many centuries the records of government activities were largely handwritten and produced one at a time in scriveners' houses.[5] As a rule, there were few copies of each document. Most documents were posted in convenient public places for general viewing, then housed in archives for reference.[6] As mechanized publishing increased the number of document copies and the speed with which identical copies could be produced, the distribution of public information about government became more widespread[7] Mass communication technology provided for mass information distribution. Everyone who could read, or could be read to, could be informed about government activity.[8]

Communication theorists commonly divide the discussion around mass media into eras known as the first and second media ages.[9] The "first age" is denoted as communication from one to many with centralized controls, often through the state government, and usually emphasizes one-way communication. Generally speaking, twentieth-century broadcast platforms provide an example of this "first age." Earlier historical periods in which governments licensed publishers are similar, though less familiar to modern communication.

The "second age" is usually one of communication from many speakers to many receivers, encouraging two-way communication, and often less controlled by government and therefore facilitating political engagement because of its more equal accessibility. The explosion of media platforms using the World Wide Web, as well as cloud-based activities of the twenty-first century, are the examples that theorists point to for modeling and theory building.

The expectation of public scrutiny and government accountability, however, are evident through both the first and second communication media ages whenever the social framework of representative democracies is reviewed. Scholars note this expectation each time political communication theorists map new models for current environments. In an overview of the history of communication theory, David Holmes summarized in his introduction to *Communication Theory: Media, Technology and Society* that the modern era of digital communication offers "free-ranging possibilities of political expression and rights of electronic assembly which encounter far fewer constraints, whether technical, political or social."[10]

While media platforms are not the foundation of government structure, scholars often attribute the success of democracy to a robust and open communication framework.[11] Cyberspace is often seen today as a renewal of the public sphere for open discussion and wide dispersal of public information.[12] Some media enthusiasts such as *Wired* magazine's Kevin Kelly overtly characterized this second media age as forwarding "Thomas Jefferson's 200-year-old dream of thinking individuals self-actualizing a democracy."[13]

Theory in Practice

What is most important to the work of this book is the basic expectation within a representative democracy that officeholders should provide information about their government to those on whose behalf they labor. As we look more closely at the details of what the U.S. Constitution's authors constructed, we find that the intention was not just to provide documentation but also to encourage participation and engagement at the constituent level with the activities that leadership initiated.

The evidence for this inference is in the particulars of the Constitution itself, but also in the notes that James Madison reported from the debates during the federal convention of 1787 when the Constitution was drafted.[14] Since these notes were not taken directly during the meetings themselves, but instead were reconstructed from Madison's recollections each day after the meetings, there will always be some skepticism about their accuracy. In general, however, they provide an outline of the concerns and arguments offered for many components of the newly fashioned government at that time.

To contextualize the highlights of these debates, it is important to remember that the 1776 Declaration of Independence and the 1777 Articles of Confederation, ratified in 1781, preceded the work done on the federal constitution. All of the member states had constitutions of their own, and so the work of drafting a more encompassing document for the federation was not wholly new to the delegates. Yet the issues and details were often discussed vigorously and in some cases vehemently. The debates were not confined to the formal caucuses. Personal letters and newspaper editorials authored by colonials were often outspoken on the need to encourage public engagement if the new government were to function as an improvement on the British constitution.

John Adams, of Massachusetts, wrote in 1774 to fellow delegate George Read, of Maryland, about a meeting he had had with a mutual colleague from Virginia, Patrick Henry. "I had with Mr. Henry, before we took leave of each other, some familiar conversation, in which I expressed a full conviction that our resolves, declaration of rights, enumeration of wrongs, petitions, remonstrances, and addresses, associations and non-importation agreements, however they might be expected in America, and however necessary to cement the union of the colonies, would be but waste paper in England. Mr. Henry said they might make some impression among the people of England, but agreed with me that they would be totally lost upon the government."[15]

Figure 1.1 "The Manner in which the American Colonies Declared themselves Independant of the King of England, throughout the different Provinces on July 4, 1776," *Bernard's New Complete Authentic History of England*, courtesy of the William L. Clements Library, University of Michigan.

Among those resolutions noted in Adams's letter about the 1774 Continental Congress was "That the foundation of English liberty and of all free government, is a right in the people to participate in their legislative council."[16] The members of Congress also prepared and sent a letter to "The Inhabitants of the Province of Quebec" that encouraged an alliance with the like-minded by listing those aspects of life in America that were important to a better government.

> The last right we shall mention, regards the freedom of the press. The importance of this consists, besides the advancement of truth, science and morality, the arts in general, in its diffusion of liberal sentiments on the administration of government, its ready communication of thoughts between subjects, and its consequential promotion of union among them, whereby oppressive officers are shamed or intimidated into more honourable and just modes of conducting affairs.[17]

The Continental Congress interrupted its work while some members prepared to challenge the British government more formally. Two dozen of the delegates signed the Declaration of Independence, joined by more than two dozen others who were not delegates to the congress. Only two of the original 1774 members of Congress would sign both the declaration and serve in the subsequent constitutional convention: Roger Sherman of Connecticut and George Read of Delaware.

Figure 1.2. "A Gazette Extraordinary from Berkeley Square," from British Satire Collection 1782–1796, courtesy of the William L. Clements Library, University of Michigan.

Already important to the member states at the time of independence was the necessity of public records as evident in the Declaration's lines 38 and 39. "He [King of Great Britain] has called together legislative bodies at places unusual, uncomfortable, and distant from the depository of public records, for the sole purpose…." And near the end of the 121-line document, the authors and signators of the Declaration emphasize the importance of public documents by closing with the following statement:

> We, therefore, the representatives of the United States of America, in general Congress assembled…solemnly publish and declare, that these united colonies are, and of right ought to be, free and independent states….[18]

Close on the heels of the Declaration of Independence came the formation of a government to bind the member colonies that had declared themselves states. That set of 13 articles provided for the protection of states' rights among the confederation and identified only those elements of government delegated to the group as a congress of the whole. Article Four specifically notes that "Full faith and credit shall be given in each of these States to the records, acts and judicial proceedings," thereby valuing the official documents along with states' laws and court activity as worthy of specific mention and protection.[19]

Article Nine contains the essence of congressional rights and responsibilities and details specifically how disagreements between the states shall be adjudicated by Congress. This codification begins with line 205:

> Whenever the legislative or executive authority or lawful agent of any state in controversy with another shall present a petition to Congress stating the matter in question and praying for a hearing, notice thereof shall be given by order of Congress to the legislative or executive authority of the other State in the controversy….

Nearly forty lines were dedicated to describing how the panel of commissioners or judges would be constituted and how the proceedings would be handled. And when a decision about the controversy was reached, that judgment would be "lodged among the acts of Congress for the security of the parties concerned…," which meant that the outcome would become part of the public records kept by Congress.[20]

And then to make it clear that Congress was not allowed to act in secrecy or without public review, the closing paragraph of Article Nine directed that

> The Congress of the United States…shall publish the journal of their proceedings monthly, except such parts thereof relating to treaties, alliances or military operations,

> as in their judgment require secrecy, and the yeas and nays of the delegates of each State on any question shall be entered on the journal, when it is desired by any delegate; and the delegates of a State, or any of them, at his or their request, shall be furnished with a transcript of the said journal, except such parts as are above excepted, to lay before the legislatures of the several States.[21]

Clearly, the Articles' framers were concerned with transparency of the federal government and severely limited what could be kept from public review. And not only were the journals of Congress to be published, but delegates could ask for and receive copies directed to their home-state legislatures, like a report card on delegate activity.

Similar provisions with attached rationale for inclusion could be found among several state constitutions. For example, the 1780 Massachusetts constitution included the following support for public documents: "The people... have a right to require of their lawgivers and magistrates an exact and constant observation of them, in the formation and execution of the laws necessary for the good administration of the commonwealth."[22]

Though the Articles of Confederation provided an initial framework for the federal government, it became clear after the War of Independence was fought and won that some elements of the young nation had not been detailed clearly enough, and some revision was required. In 1787, a half-dozen years after the ratification of the Articles, a group of delegates met to redraft a more detailed constitution. With a few years of experience now under their belts, the convention members set out to craft the newer version of their confederation.

While their government ideal would be open to public scrutiny, the debates about how such a constitution would be written concluded that it would be done in secret in order to promote open debate—thinking out loud without reprisal. James Madison, a delegate from Virginia, disobeyed the ban on convention records and kept notes at home each day, reconstructing arguments and identifying votes as he could recollect.

Madison justified his actions in his preface to the collection, which was not to be published until after his death, by noting:

> The curiosity I had felt during my researches into the History of the most distinguished Confederacies, particularly those of antiquity, and the deficiency I found in the means of satisfying it more especially in what related to the process, the principles, the reasons, & the anticipations which prevailed in the formation of them, determined me to preserve as far as I could an exact account of what might pass in the Convention whilst....[23]

The selections here from the federal convention debates are those that focus squarely on the need for public review of government work and how that would best be served. Remember that these delegates, while holding deep convictions about the benefits of a democracy, were still hashing out how that might look in a modern world. The government structures of Athens and other Greek city-states were known to the well-educated members of this congress, but none had lived in such an ideal democracy. In addition, many of those who had come together to redraft the Constitution were also deeply concerned about how a federation might best be designed around the wide variations of its member states.

Perhaps first and foremost for our discussion was the early recognition by the convention members of the power and magnitude of written records about the proceedings. Madison noted on May 29, the third day of the convention, that all agreed no copies were to be made of entries in the official convention journal without expressed leave of the membership, referred to as the House. Further, they decided that members would only be permitted to inspect the journal and that nothing spoken during the debates would be published without permission.

One delegate suggested a committee to oversee the secretary of the convention. That motion was defeated because "a committee might have an interest & bias in moulding the entry according to their opinions and wishes." According to Madison, Gouverneur Morris, of Pennsylvania, said succinctly that the "proceedings of the Convention belonged to the Secretary [Major Jackson] as their impartial officer."[24]

Concerns about the official records were raised again in August when debates centered on the inclusions for House and Senate journals to be "published from time to time."[25] Madison reported that he and John Rutledge, of South Carolina, moved that each House keep a journal of its proceedings except when secrecy was required. Several members moved to insert more specific exceptions to the journal publication rule by adding "except such as related to treaties & military operations."[26]

Nay votes overwhelmed the insertion, and the discussion moved more widely to the question of any exclusions for the published journals. Oliver Ellsworth, of Connecticut, said that "the clause was objectionable in so many shapes it may well be struck out altogether." Madison went on to report that Ellsworth added "the Legislature will not fail to publish their proceedings from time to time. The people will call for it if it should be improperly omitted."

James Wilson, of Pennsylvania, said he thought that "The people have a right to know what their Agents are doing or have done, and it should not be in the option of the Legislature to conceal their proceedings." Interestingly, there was no debate, according to Madison, about whether there should be publication of the House and Senate journals, but only what these bodies might be allowed to leave out of the official records—records that were intended for public inspection and distribution.

When it came time to vote on the addendum phrase "except such parts thereof as may in their judgment require secrecy," there was not unanimity. A majority agreed to let the House and Senate decide the specifics of what might be deemed worthy of secrecy. New Hampshire's delegates were divided on the question, with Pennsylvania, Delaware, Maryland, and South Carolina voting against inclusion of the phrase. New York and Rhode Island did not vote on the question at all, according to Madison.[27]

Another insertion into Article I of the Constitution included a requirement that "an account of the public expenditures should be annually published." Discussion followed that a complete, once-a-year report was an overwhelming task, but that shorter intervals would only lead to incomplete information. Rufus King, of Massachusetts, remarked that "Congress might indeed make a monthly publication, but it would afford no satisfactory information." Again the discussion hinged on what the constituencies would pressure the legislatures to do if reports were not forthcoming. Madison reported that ultimately the phrase "from time to time" was agreed upon as discretionary but practical.[28]

There seemed to be no discussion outside of the drafting committee meetings about the requirement that the executive branch, and the elected president specifically, would from time to time provide the legislature with information on the state of the union. The specific language of this directive came to the convention floor intact on August 6 under the name of Article X, section 2.

There seemed as well no need for discussion about the publication of judiciary opinions and case law. A centuries-long tradition of court dicta published for public review was so entrenched in the social norms of Western governments that the convention members did not spend much time detailing what should be done by the third branch of the new government. The points of contention were more significantly about the appointment of the court members and the jurisdiction of the Supreme Court.[29]

As members discussed the three branches of government and their responsibilities, there were several occasions on which a bill of rights was suggested.

Often the point of interest arose when one member or another became concerned about government transparency or government overreaching of individual liberties. For example, in the midst of discussions about legislative responsibilities for maintaining militia, Charles Pinckney, of South Carolina, submitted a list of rights on August 20 for consideration. The list included "The liberty of the Press shall be inviolably preserved" and "No soldier shall be quartered in any house in time of peace without consent of the owner," along with "No religious test or qualification shall ever be annexed to any oath of office under the authority of the U.S."[30] There was no immediate debate, and the list was referred to a committee for further discussion. Clearly the members of this congress were weighing all sorts of concerns as they discussed any particular element.

On September 12 a revised version of the Constitution was read to the House. George Mason, of Virginia, suggested the document would be better received if it were prefaced by a bill of rights. In fact, Mason added, he believed it could be produced in a few hours. Elbridge Gerry, of Massachusetts, moved for a committee to prepare a bill of rights, and Mason seconded the motion. Roger Sherman, of Connecticut, said he thought that the states' declarations of rights were sufficient and that the federal legislature would not overstep the states' jurisdiction. Mason interjected that the federal laws would be paramount to the states' bills of rights. And so the question was called, and voted down.[31]

Again, two days later, Pinckney and Gerry moved to insert a clause among the Article I legislative powers that would declare "the liberty of the Press should be inviolably observed." Roger Sherman, of Connecticut, retorted that such a clause was unnecessary, as "The power of Congress does not extend to the Press." Again the motion failed.[32] Time and again the movement to include a bill of rights, particularly one that protected communication among constituents from government intervention, was obviously on the minds of many House members. Apparently, however, the convention as a whole believed it was unnecessary to provide this sort of legal protection when everyone already understood its value and social necessity.

At the end of the constitutional convention in mid-September, Rufus King suggested that the journals of the convention should either be destroyed or deposited with George Washington, who had been unanimously elected and served as president of the convention. King's concern, according to Madison, was that if the contents of the journals were made public, "a bad use would be made of them by those who would wish to prevent the adoption of the Constitution."[33]

Another member suggested that destroying the journals might be preferable in the short run, but "as false suggestions may be propagated, it should not be impossible to contradict them," and so favored at least a temporary repository. In the end the House agreed that the papers of the convention would be left in the hands of Washington until other orders were rendered by the new Congress, "if [it is] ever formed under the Constitution."[34]

Offering the Constitution for ratification presented an early opportunity to test the expectations of political engagement, as nearly every public newspaper published copies for distribution to subscribers and neighbors alike. A collection of pamphlets published between 1787 and 1788 by one Richard Henry Lee, writing as the "Federal Farmer of Virginia," captures the spirited discussions across the states. Lee was not just a pamphleteer. He had served as a member of the Continental Congress and signed the Declaration of Independence.

> Men who wish the people of this country to determine for themselves, and deliberately to fit the government to their situation, must feel some degree of indignation at those attempts to hurry the adoption of a system, and to shut the door against examination. The very attempts create suspicions, that those who make them have secret views, or see some defects in the system, which, in the hurry of affairs, they expect will escape the eye of a free people.... What can be the views of those gentlemen in Boston, who countenanced the Printers in shutting up the press against a fair and free investigation of this important system in the usual way.... If the constitution presented be a good one, it will stand the test with a well informed people.[35]

The purpose of this extended review of the U.S. constitutional convention is to draw attention to a simple observation. During the drafting of the U.S. Constitution, there was little discussion about whether there should be public records, public notice, or public review of the government's work. Instead the discussion was about ensuring limits on the kinds of things that government could and should keep secret.

Congress would, of course, provide journals of legislative activity; the Executive branch would, of course, provide information regularly about how the nation was doing under the laws passed by Congress; and the Judiciary would, of course, publish court opinions as they were decided so that everyone understood the details of the laws enacted by Congress and enforced by the executive branch.

The norms of access to government information came easily to the American shores and played out in a series of cases once the new nation was formed. The foundation for some of the case law can be found as early as 1372 when the

English Parliament required that court records be made available to anyone in need of the information in them.[36] Subsequent court rulings based on English common law allowed taxpayers access to public records "without shewing... whether they [the records] relate directly to the point in question or not."[37]

Though U.S. laws were taking shape around the English common law traditions, courts still occasionally cited the English law to support access to government-held information.[38] A 1900 Indiana case stated directly that "The general rule which obtained at common law was that every person was entitled to an inspection of public records, by himself or agent, provided he had an interest in the matters to which such records related."[39] A Michigan court was even more strident about public access to government-held information in 1928 when writing, "If there be any rule of the English common law that denies the public the right of access to public records, it is repugnant to the spirit of our democratic institutions.... There is no question as to the common-law right of the people at large to inspect public documents and records."[40]

More Recent Examples

The United States was not alone in the expectations of government transparency. Representative democracies that more specifically have become federal republics exist by the dozens.[41] For example, Switzerland declared itself a confederation in 1848 with a renewed declaration in 1874. A revised constitution in 1999 included a number of articles that support and require open communication among government officials and the electorate as a means of engaging the electorate with the governing process.[42]

Similarly, Germany declared itself a federal republic in 1918, and the forerunner of its current constitution was adopted in 1949. The most recent revision begins with a long list of basic rights for its citizens that includes free speech, assembly, and association, as well privacy for letters and telecommunication.[43] The Swiss constitution also guarantees a free press, radio, and television, as well as editorial secrecy, and prohibits government censorship.[44]

More specifically, in the German constitution's chapters for government duties and obligations, Article 42 says specifically: "True and accurate reports on the public meetings of the House of Representatives and of its committees does not give rise to any liability,"[45] providing for something like a free-press, watchdog function. Article 43 goes on to instruct that "members of the Senate and the Government as well as persons commissioned by them have access to all meetings of the House of Representatives and its committees," indicating that there will be no secret gatherings.

Lithuania, a self-declared democratic republic since 1990, adopted a citizen's right to be informed and a duty on the part of the state to publish official announcements. The Lithuanian constitution requires in Article 25 that "Citizens shall have the right to obtain any available information which concerns them from State agencies in the manner established by law."[46] Subsequent laws have reinforced this. A 1996 group of laws includes the unequivocal article, "State and municipal institutions and agencies must inform the public of their activities," and Article 21 warns that "Refusal to publish official state announcements...shall incur liability in accordance with the procedure established by the law."[47]

Even countries that are not, strictly speaking, representative democracies attend to public notice as a core legal concept. For example, New Zealand, whose form of government comes out of the long traditions of British law, provides that public notice "is to be published in the official Gazette, or in one or more newspapers circulating in the place or district to which the act, matter, or thing required to be published relates or refers, or...arises."[48] One such example is the list of active businesses registered in the country. Additions to and removals from that list are to be advertised as a public notice.[49]

National constitutions are not the only forum for implementing government transparency and engaging the membership. International treaties, legislation, and case law have included requirements for public notice of these global networks' activities. As recently as 2012, the European Court of Justice's Fourth Chamber found that Ireland failed to fulfill its obligations as a member state when it did not provide public notice to affected communities about environmentally sensitive projects and would therefore be fined substantial sums until that was rectified.[50] Also common in many of the European Union Directives is a section that requires public notice of proposed changes or public works. The articles often look something like this example from the 1985 "Assessment of the effects of certain public and private projects on the environment"[51] directive:

Article 1

2. Member States shall ensure that:
   - any request for development consent and any information gathered pursuant to Article 5 are made available to the public,
   - the public concerned is given the opportunity to express an opinion before the project is initiated.

3. The detailed arrangements for such information and consultation shall be determined by the Member States, which may in particular, depending on the particular characteristics of the projects or sites concerned:
   - determine the public concerned,
   - specify the places where the information can be consulted,
   - specify the way in which the public may be informed, for example by bill-posting within a certain radius, publication in local newspapers, organization of exhibitions with plans, drawings, tables, graphs, models,
   - determine the manner in which the public is to be consulted, for example, by written submissions, by public enquiry,
   - fix appropriate time limits for the various stages of the procedure in order to ensure that a decision is taken within a reasonable period.

If the project needs to forego public notice, then the state must provide the following to the EU:

Article 2

1. Member States shall adopt all measures necessary to ensure that, before consent is given, projects likely to have significant effects on the environment by virtue inter alia, of their nature, size or location are made subject to an assessment with regard to their effects. These projects are defined in Article 4.
2. The environmental impact assessment may be integrated into the existing procedures for consent to projects in the Member States, or, failing this, into other procedures or into procedures to be established to comply with the aims of this Directive.
3. Member States may, in exceptional cases, exempt a specific project in whole or in part from the provisions laid down in this Directive. In this event, the Member States shall:
   (a) consider whether another form of assessment would be appropriate and whether the information thus collected should be made available to the public;
   (b) make available to the public concerned the information relating to the exemption and the reasons for granting it;
   (c) inform the Commission, prior to granting consent, of the reasons justifying the exemption granted, and provide it with the information made available, where appropriate, to their own nationals.

> The Commission shall immediately forward the documents received to the other Member States.
> The Commission shall report annually to the Council on the application of this paragraph.

Social Triple Helix

Returning, then, to our elements of political theory, the language found in the U.S. Constitution, for example, might be said to focus on detailing the social process. These elements are:

- the elections of legislators and the executive, as well as appointment of judiciary by those elected involving cooperation among those with power,
- the three branches of government sharing responsibilities,
- then, leading to decision making for the group,
- which then enhances the activities and benefits of the federation for all citizens in good standing.

The specifics of international case law and treaty directives similarly emphasize a social process of public notice in order to inform the elected or appointed bureaucrats who must cooperate in their power sharing in order to enhance the lives of all who are members of the federation.

The relationship and interplay of these elements requires cooperation within a social process of elections that must be accepted by winners and losers. The temporary bestowing of power through elections requires that legislators must work not only with each other but also with their constituents and the administrative branch to facilitate group decision making. And then all members must agree to abide by the decisions. Now, as it was hundreds of years ago, a democracy continues to be a complicated network for government constructs.

Representative democracies can only thrive where the means of communication are clear, vigorous, trusted, and true to the intents and purposes of the law devised by the electorate. The U.S. federal convention of 1787 that drafted a revised Constitution from the Articles of Confederation understood the importance of unabashed debate to its task, and it sought ways to protect that conversation as well as move a nation forward. The members understood, too, that what worked for the convention was not isolated, but must continue as the backbone of their social network. Records must be systematically kept and shared liberally if the social conversation is to keep the nation alive.[52]

The avenues of collection and distribution of public documents vary from nation to nation, but there are a few common mechanisms. For example, public attention most often goes to freedom of access laws, referred to as FOI or FOA, that require government to keep records for review and to provide copies when called upon by constituents. FOI laws can be found among every active representative democracy, and the value of these legal instruments is undisputed.[53] But public notice, as an instrument of government-to-constituent communication, has been a central, though unheralded, part of the representative democracies around the world. Community newspapers, an early means of posting and circulating these notices, were but one of the ways of getting information about government work out to the electorate.[54]

While FOI laws often describe what must be kept and provided, they also require that constituents seek out the information from government.[55] Public notice, on the other hand, requires that government provide information in the form of reports, budgets, calls for action, and action taken without the public requesting these details at each phase of the activity, day in and day out. In fact, the regularity and continuity of reporting these sorts of government activities in most working democracies is so much a part of public life that few would ask the question, "Why distribute public notices?" What we are now asking in this book is rather how best to distribute these public notices.

What makes public notice conceptually more useful than FOI is simply the difference between asking for things and having them delivered without asking. Freedom of information laws usually put the burden on citizens to ask specifically for what is desired among government documents, and then to pay for the time and cost of fulfilling that request. Public notice, on the other hand, requires that information be made available without the public even asking. In fact, the government is not only required to make information available, but must publish it or post it in some prominent place such as a widely circulated newspaper, on a town square bulletin board, or on the web.

The only requirement of the public is to specify by law what kinds of subject matter need to be made public—a class of information, if you will—rather than make ad hoc requests for specific documents. The result of this process of specifying by law an entire class of documents means that public notices are about everything from property seizures to town budgets to ordinance changes across time. By contrast, FOI documents are about property seizures, for example, within a certain district, or for a certain period of time, or of a certain value described in the request for documents.

These postings of government activity reports that result from public notice, therefore, make it possible for public browsing. Citizens are free to learn about what government is doing, even if they didn't know they needed to know or wanted to know about the change in downtown zoning, the county budget line changes, or the storage lockers that the state police have seized. These are just a few of the examples that are available to anyone casually reading the classified pages of many local newspapers or the websites that are hosted with public access.[56]

Figure 1.3 "The Great Negro Emancipation." *Harper's Weekly*, December 20, 1862, p. 816, courtesy of the William L. Clements Library, University of Michigan.

These notices make it possible for anyone to see not only what government is doing today, but also to look back across time to see what government has done similarly or differently in the same sort of activity without asking permission from anyone. All that is necessary is access to the posting environment—a newspaper that is archived, a website that remains static, or a bulletin board that never removes notices.

Figure 1.4 "Pickets Fraternizing over Coffee and Exchanging Papers." *Harper's Weekly*, July 26, 1862, courtesy of the William L. Clements Library, University of Michigan.

Public Notice in the Twenty-First Century

In the world of modern social media, public notice has taken on a new life in the ways that it might come to us. With the onset of a "second age" of communication (noted earlier in this chapter), many expect government documents to be available on demand, where once those documents were available on a fixed publication schedule. Public notice items that once appeared as tiny-type, paid advertisements in the local daily newspaper are now posted, without much guidance, wherever government bureaucrats can find cheap space on a server. This change in attitude about the process of posting notices and the expectations about availability and accessibility by modern information consumers has begun to shift the framework of distribution for much of what government provides the electorate. What was once regular as clockwork through a cooperative of public offices and newspaper edit desks, tear sheets, and publication schedules, is now available whenever a public office administrator learns the upload and download routines of the bureau's software.

Legislatures are where public notice laws originate, and the courts are where those laws are adjudicated. It is within these two bodies that changes in these laws are beginning to reflect the modern desire to post government information on wider platforms such as the World Wide Web as well as the timeliness and access to these notices. As of 2011 in the United States, the largest group of state court decisions clustered around the issue of defining what constituted public notice content. And at least 19 states, with 34 statutes, provided for some clarification about what constituted a public notice, also referred to as a legal notice.[57]

However, these statutes and opinions did not dissuade legislatures from offering changes to many aspects of public notice laws. There were at least 18 bills in 15 states in the 2010 and 2011 legislative cycles aimed at changing the format, timeliness, or availability of legal notices, and many of them included website use in place of existing newspaper publication practices. There were fewer—perhaps only two—offering similar changes for the states' statutes around another term sometimes used for public notice: "official notice."[58]

As local governments feel their way toward amending or repurposing public notice functions into a World Wide Web environment, there are plenty of questions to be asked and answered along the route to developing better protocols for such a vastly different publication environment. After all, websites and search engines make it possible for the curious, pajama-clad web lurkers in Russia to learn about the notices of abandoned property in Arizona, or distant relatives in Canada to search the death notices in Florida.[59] While the particulars of posting and refreshing those posts—including access and accuracy, storage and retrieval, and cost and sustainability—are all important details, it is essential at the outset to understand and remember the context for and uses of public notice as a social function.

This chapter has established the social need of public notice within the government framework of representative democracies. While public notice is often accompanied by freedom of access, it is public notice alone that requires government to provide—without requests or pleas, and in a timely and intelligible format—information about what it is about to do or has done to its constituents. Public notice laws and political expectations are what require a government to keep records of what it is doing, or has done, and it is public notice that systematically, regularly, and fully reports to the electorate what that government plans to do, or has done on behalf of those for whom it works.

What happens now that so much of the government's output is in digital form, where once it was in paper documents that could be collected and filed in folders, thumbtacked to a wall, or published as a handbill? What happens when digital posting occurs in corners of the web where few citizens surf or lurk? What happens when public records are jumbled or lost because of software and hardware migrations? And what can government and we as citizens do to safeguard our collective memory about what we approved or what was done on our behalf?

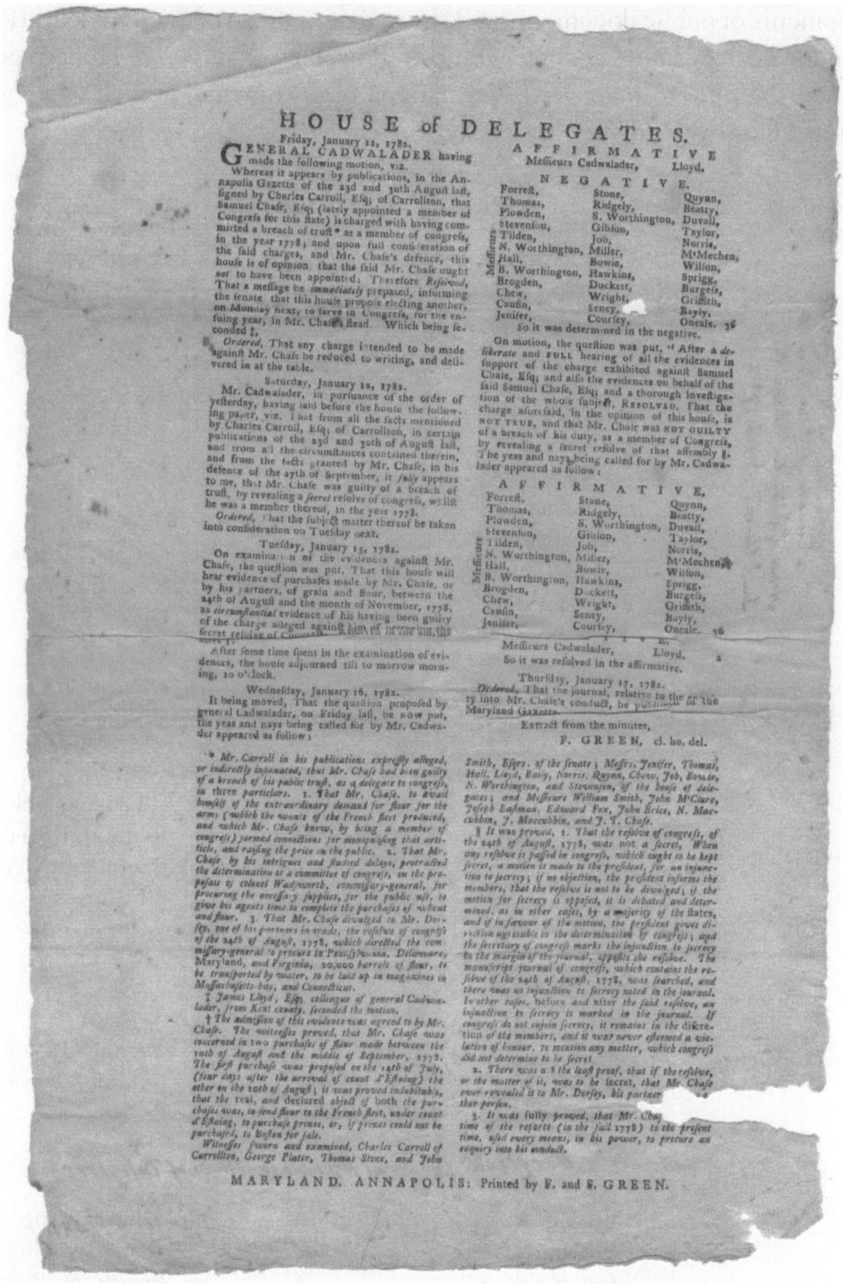

HOUSE of DELEGATES.

Friday, January 11, 1782.

GENERAL CADWALADER having made the following motion, viz.

Whereas it appears by publications, in the Annapolis Gazette of the 23d and 30th August last, signed by Charles Carroll, Esq; of Carrollton, that Samuel Chase, Esq; (lately appointed a member of Congress for this state) is charged with having committed a breach of trust * as a member of congress, in the year 1778; and upon full consideration of the said charges, and Mr. Chase's defence, this house is of opinion that the said Mr. Chase ought *not* to have been appointed: Therefore *Resolved*, That a message be *immediately* prepared, informing the senate that this house propose electing another, on Monday next, to serve in Congress, for the ensuing year, in Mr. Chase's stead. Which being seconded ‡,

Ordered, That any charge intended to be made against Mr. Chase be reduced to writing, and delivered in at the table.

Saturday, January 12, 1782.

Mr. Cadwalader, in pursuance of the order of yesterday, having laid before the house the following paper, viz. That from all the facts mentioned by Charles Carroll, Esq; of Carrollton, in certain publications of the 23d and 30th of August last, and from all the circumstances contained therein, and from the facts granted by Mr. Chase, in his defence of the 27th of September, it *fully* appears to me, that Mr. Chase was guilty of a breach of trust, by revealing a *secret* resolve of congress, whilst he was a member thereof, in the year 1778.

Ordered, That the subject matter thereof be taken into consideration on Tuesday next.

Tuesday, January 15, 1782.

On examination of the evidences against Mr. Chase, the question was put, That this house will hear evidence of purchases made by Mr. Chase, or by his partners, of grain and flour, between the 24th of August and the month of November, 1778, as *circumstantial* evidence of his having been guilty of the charge alleged against him of betraying the secret resolve of Congress. Resolved in the affirmative †.

After some time spent in the examination of evidences, the house adjourned till to morrow morning, 10 o'clock.

Wednesday, January 16, 1782.

It being moved, That the question proposed by general Cadwalader, on Friday last, be NOW put, the yeas and nays being called for by Mr. Cadwalader appeared as follow:

A F F I R M A T I V E

Messieurs Cadwalader, Lloyd.

N E G A T I V E.

Messieurs

Forrest,	Stone,	Quynn,
Thomas,	Ridgely,	Beatty,
Plowden,	S. Worthington,	Duvall,
Stevenson,	Gibson,	Taylor,
Tilden,	Job,	Norris,
N. Worthington,	Miller,	M'Mechen,
Hall,	Bowie,	Wilson,
B. Worthington,	Hawkins,	Sprigg,
Brogden,	Duckett,	Burgess,
Chew,	Wright,	Griffith,
Causin,	Seney,	Bayly,
Jenifer,	Coursey,	Oneale. 36

So it was determined in the negative.

On motion, the question was put, "After a *deliberate* and FULL hearing of all the evidences in support of the charge exhibited against Samuel Chase, Esq; and also the evidences on behalf of the said Samuel Chase, Esq; and a thorough investigation of the whole subject, RESOLVED, That the charge aforesaid, in the opinion of this house, is NOT TRUE, and that Mr. Chase was NOT GUILTY of a breach of his duty, as a member of Congress, by revealing a secret resolve of that assembly ‖. The yeas and nays being called for by Mr. Cadwalader appeared as follow:

A F F I R M A T I V E.

Messieurs

Forrest,	Stone,	Quynn,
Thomas,	Ridgely,	Beatty,
Plowden,	S. Worthington,	Duvall,
Stevenson,	Gibson,	Taylor,
Tilden,	Job,	Norris,
N. Worthington,	Miller,	M'Mechen,
Hall,	Bowie,	Wilson,
B. Worthington,	Hawkins,	Sprigg,
Brogden,	Duckett,	Burgess,
Chew,	Wright,	Griffith,
Causin,	Seney,	Bayly,
Jenifer,	Coursey,	Oneale. 36

N E G A T I V E.

Messieurs Cadwalader, Lloyd. 2

So it was resolved in the affirmative.

Thursday, January 17, 1782.

Ordered, That the journal, relative to the enquiry into Mr. Chase's conduct, be published in the Maryland Gazette.

Extract from the minutes,

F. GREEN, cl. ho. del.

* *Mr. Carroll in his publications expressly alleged, or indirectly insinuated, that Mr. Chase had been guilty of a breach of his public trust, as a delegate to congress, in three particulars. 1. That Mr. Chase, to avail himself of the extraordinary demand for flour for the army (which the wants of the French fleet produced, and which Mr. Chase knew, by being a member of congress) formed connections for monopolising that article, and raising the price on the public. 2. That Mr. Chase by his intrigues and studied delays, protracted the determination of a committee of congress, on the proposals of colonel Wadsworth, commissary-general, for procuring the necessary supplies, for the public use, to give his agents time to complete the purchases of wheat and flour. 3. That Mr. Chase divulged to Mr. Dorsey, one of his partners in trade, the resolve of congress of the 24th of August, 1778, which directed the commissary-general to procure in Pennsylvania, Delaware,* Maryland, *and Virginia,* 20,000 *barrels of flour, to be transported by water, to be laid up in magazines in Massachusetts-bay, and Connecticut.*

‡ *James Lloyd, Esq; colleague of general Cadwalader, from Kent county, seconded the motion.*

† *The admission of this evidence was agreed to by Mr. Chase. The witnesses proved, that Mr. Chase was concerned in* two *purchases of flour made between the 10th of August and the middle of September, 1778. The first purchase was proposed on the 14th of July, (four days after the arrival of count d'Estaing) the other on the 10th of August; it was proved indubitably, that the* real, *and* declared *object of* both *the purchases was, to send flour to the French fleet, under count d'Estaing, to purchase prizes, or, if prizes could not be purchased, to Boston for sale.*

Witnesses sworn and examined, Charles Carroll of Carrollton, George Plater, Thomas Stone, and John Smith, Esqrs. of the senate; Messrs. Jenifer, Thomas, Hall, Lloyd, Baily, Norris, Quynn, Chew, Job, Bowie, N. Worthington, and Stevenson, of the house of delegates; and Messieurs William Smith, John M'Clure, Joseph Eastman, Edward Fox, John Brice, N. Maccubbin, J. Maccubbin, and J. T. Chase.

‖ *It was proved,* 1. *That the resolve of congress, of the 24th of August, 1778, was* not *a secret. When any resolve is passed in congress, which ought to be kept secret, a motion is made to the president, for an injunction to secrecy; if no objection, the president informs the members, that the resolve is not to be divulged; if the motion for secrecy is opposed, it is debated and determined, as in other cases, by a majority of the states, and if in favour of the motion, the president gives direction agreeable to the determination of congress; and the secretary of congress marks the injunction to secrecy in the margin of the journal, opposite the resolve. The manuscript journal of congress, which contains the resolve of the 24th of August, 1778, was searched, and there was no injunction to secrecy noted in the journal. In other cases,* before *and* after *the said resolve, an injunction to secrecy is marked in the journal. If congress do not enjoin secrecy, it remains in the discretion of the members, and it was never esteemed a violation of honour, to mention any matter, which congress did not determine to be secret.*

2. *There was not the least proof, that if the resolve, or the matter of it, was to be secret, that Mr. Chase ever revealed it to Mr. Dorsey, his partner [illegible] other person.*

3. *It was* fully *proved, that Mr. Cha[illegible] time of the reports (in the fall 1778) to the present time, used every means, in his power, to procure an enquiry into his conduct.*

MARYLAND. ANNAPOLIS: Printed by F. and S. GREEN.

Figure 1.5 "House of Delegates, Friday, January 11, 1782," Maryland General Assembly Broadsides, small, courtesy of the William L. Clements Library, University of Michigan.

The next several chapters will provide in greater detail the historical developments of public documents and the commonalities of modern definitions of public notice. Those chapters will be followed by examples of modern governments' efforts to manage the avalanche of documents, as well as suggestions for improvements in those systems.

[i] **Bold** indicates membership in more than one column of names.

	1774 Continental Congress	Declaration of Independence	Constitutional Convention
New Hampshire	John Sullivan, Nathaniel Folsom	Josiah Bartlett, William Whipple, Matthew Thornton	John Langdon, Nicholas Gilman
Massachusetts Bay	**John Adams, Samuel Adams,** Thomas Cushing, **Robert Treat Paine**	**John Adams, Samuel Adams,** John Hancock, **Robert Treat Paine, Elbridge Gerry**	Nathaniel Gorham, Rufus King, **Elbridge Gerry**, Caleb Strong
Rhode Island	**Stephen Hopkins,** Samuel Ward	**Stephen Hopkins,** William Ellery	
Connecticut	Eliphalet Dyer, **Roger Sherman,** Silas Deane	Samuel Huntington, **Roger Sherman,** William Williams, Oliver Wolcott	William Samuel Johnson, **Roger Sherman,** Oliver Ellsworth
New York	Isaac Low, John Alsop, John Jay, **Philip Livingston,** James Duane, **William Floyd,** Henry Wisner, Simon Boerum	Lewis Morris, **Philip Livingston,** Francis Lewis, **William Floyd**	Alexander Hamilton, John Lansing, Robert Yates
New Jersey	James Kinsey, **William Livingston,** Stephen Crane, Richard Smith, John De Hart	Abraham Clark, John Hart, Francis Hopkins, Richard Stockton, John Witherspoon	**William Livingston,** David Brearly, William Paterson, Jonathan Dayton, William Houston

	1774 Continental Congress	Declaration of Independence	Constitutional Convention
Pennsylvania	Joseph Galloway, John Dickinson, Charles Humphreys, **Thomas Mifflin**, Edward Biddle, **John Morton, George Ross**	**George Clymer, Ben Franklin, Robert Morris, John Morton,** Benjamin Rush, **George Ross,** James Smith, **James Wilson,** George Taylor	**Benjamin Franklin, Thomas Mifflin, Robert Morris, George Clymer**, Thomas FitzSimons, Jared Ingersoll, **James Wilson,** Gouverneur Morris
Delaware	**Caesar Rodney, Thomas McKean, George Read**	**George Read, Caesar Rodney, Thomas McKean**	**George Read,** Gunning Bedford, Jr., John Dickinson, Richard Bassett, Jacob Broom
Maryland	Matthew Tilghman, Thomas Johnson, William Paca, **Samuel Chase,** Robert Goldsborough	Charles Carroll, **Samuel Chase,** Thomas Stone, William Paca	James McHenry, Daniel of St. Thomas Jenifer, Daniel Carroll, Luther Martin, John Mercer
Virginia	Peyton Randolph, **Richard Henry Lee, George Washington,** Patrick Henry, Richard Bland, **Benjamin Harrison,** Edmund Pendleton	**Richard Henry Lee,** Francis Lightfoot Lee, Carter Braxton, **Benjamin Harrison,** Thomas Jefferson, **George Wythe,** Thomas Nelson	John Blair, James Madison, **George Washington,** George Mason, James McClurg, Edmund Randolph, **George Wythe**
North Carolina	**William Hooper, Joseph Hewes,** Richard Caswell	**William Hooper,** John Penn, **Joseph Hewes**	William Blount, Richard Dobbs Spaight, Hugh Williamson, William R. Davie, Alexander Martin

	1774 Continental Congress	Declaration of Independence	Constitutional Convention
South Carolina	Henry Middleton, **Thomas Lynch, Jr.**, Christopher Gadsden, **John Rutledge, Edward Rutledge**	**Edward Rutledge**, Arthur Middleton, **Thomas Lynch, Jr.**, Thomas Heyward	**John Rutledge,** Charles Cotesworth Pinckney, Charles Pinckney, Pierce Butler
Georgia		Lyman Hall, Button Gwinnett, George Walton	William Few, Abraham Baldwin

· 2 ·

THE ORIGINS OF PUBLIC NOTICE

The concept of public notice requires an initial understanding of the difference between what is socially or politically considered public and what might be thought of as private information. This distinction has been problematic for centuries, but the need for public information provided by government in representative democracies has also been taken for granted for just as long. This chapter will untangle some aspects of the delineations between public and private, and then highlight the various ways in which notice is proffered.

For an interesting summary that includes many photographs of public notices, see the illustrated history by Maurice Rickards, entitled *The Public Notice*, which provides a British overview.[60] In this work, Rickards describes not only those instances when government issued stern warnings but also includes many examples of the phrase "public notice" being used by private interests to lend an air of authority to the text. The author suggests that the history of community public notice springs from the early commands of kings and other rulers who sent messages to outlying communities. This intelligence was often read from a script and then posted somewhere for effect, if not actual reading. These edicts may also have been part of the recitation of town criers, who were charged with delivering the orders of the day. The posted document, however, was the most tangible artifact of government for those outside the physical space of the authorities, and so public notice was often a secondhand but potent devise for authority.[61]

For various layers of government, as well as those who wanted to be sure attention was paid to their particular proclamations, public notice became the vehicle of choice for everyone and anyone who wanted to issue warnings, command obedience, or just make something generally known. The ubiquity of these instances colors and confuses the public notion of public notice. This blending of official and quasi-official, however, provides an opportunity to reassess what we, as information consumers and members of social governments, want to have included in government notifications.

Figure 2.1 Public Notice posted on trees in the town center of Banja Luka, Bosnia-Herzegovina, 1999. Photo by Shannon E. Martin.

The concept of public notice in the realm of the government has a number of close relatives. One variant is *actual* or *express notice*, in which information from government is delivered directly and unequivocally to the affected parties. Another is *constructive notice*, in which due diligence would and should have informed an affected party about some government action. These terms and their definitions are found in a number of sovereign legal systems around the world. What we are most concerned with here, though, is what constitutes the quality of information emanating from government to non-government constituents so that it is deemed public information, and when that information is deemed worthy of official presentation.

Public and Private

Public, in its most elementary form, means simply the aggregate of the citizens of a state. That which is public pertains to the whole community. The word comes from the Latin *publicus*, blended with *poplicus*, meaning of the people, from *populous*, for people, and *pubes*, for adult.[62] This is usually paired as an antonym with private.

Private often suggests the opposite of public, usually in the sense that it is describing something not to be revealed to the public, or something that is not part of the public community. In Latin, again, the word comes from *privatus*, which means withdrawn from public life, and from *privus*, meaning single or individual.[63] The Latin origins help us to understand why we so fundamentally contrast private with public. However, there are some important variants of what it means to be private that have created conflicting meanings in the realm of public life and, as a result, caused confusion in the law.

In the legal sense, private means it is "not official," or something "not clothed in office."[64] Private individuals are usually those who are acting not as government officials but, more simply, as individuals. Information, however, is not so easily distinguished. Private information may be that which is kept from the government or society in general. It might also be information that has been surrendered for a number of reasons but is expected to be kept from public access or distribution.

The conditions of the public and the private dichotomy vary from one social organization to the next, as is evident in the way in which at least one county in America chose to enforce a public decision. The journal of the September 22, 1774, Continental Congress enacted the following resolutions, which individual communities adopted in various ways.

> *Resolved unanimously*, that the Congress request the Merchants and others in the several Colonies, not to send to Great Britain any orders for goods, and to direct the execution of all orders already sent to be delayed or suspended until the sense of the Congress on the means to be taken for the preservation of the liberties of America is made public.
>
> *Ordered*, that this resolution be made public by handbills, and by publishing in the newspapers.
>
> The Committee appointed to state the rights, and of the Colonies, having brought in a report of the rights, the same was read, and the consideration of it referred till Saturday next.
>
> *Ordered*, that a copy of this report be made out for each Colony.[65]

The citizens of New Castle County in Delaware were apparently willing to blend the public and private, individually identifying information if it served what some thought was a community good. When the governments of the Eastern Seaboard were determined to thwart a British tax by ceasing to import goods, the resolution was hard for some to accept. But it was reported that on August 17, 1769, "these patriot citizens mutually promise, declare and agree, upon their word of honor [to the import stoppage].... And that any one of us who shall willfully break this agreement shall have his name published in the public newspapers as a betrayer of the civil rights of America."[66] Public shaming over a personal decision, rather than actual fines, penalties, or restraints applied by the courts, seemed to be the punishment imposed.

Colonials seem to have always chafed at the arrogance of government when it decided what should be public and what should be kept from general knowledge. As an example of government attitudes toward the governed, John Adams reported the following:

> Dr. Franklin, who was known to be an active, and very able man, and to have great influence in the Province of Pennsylvania, was in Boston in the year 1754 and Mr. Shirley communicated to him the profound secret, the great design of taxing the colonies by act of Parliament. This sagacious gentleman, and distinguished patriot, to his lasting honour, sent the governor an answer in writing with the following remarks upon his scheme. Remarks which would have discouraged any honest man from the pursuit. The remarks are these.
>
> "That the people always bear the burden best, when they have, or think they have, some share in the direction.
>
> "That when public measures are generally distasteful to the people, the wheels of government must move more heavily.
>
> "That excluding the people of America from all share in the choice of a grand council for their own defense, and taxing them in Parliament, where they have no representation, would probably give extreme dissatisfaction."[67]

Franklin, ever the champion of public records and open discussion, published the following notice in a broadside dated July 7, 1803, "To the Democratic Citizens of the County of Philadelphia": "Agreeably to public notice, a number of the democratic citizens of the county of Philadelphia assembled at Wray's Inn to take 'into consideration subjects related to the ensuing election.' Resolved that the proceedings of this meeting be published in the Aurora and in Geyer's German paper."[68] Though not official government work, Franklin and others apparently thought even group discussion that might affect elections was worth publicizing.

Generally, however, in a representative democracy the government must develop a rationale for protecting this private information that has public uses. This has proven to be a difficult task. Most of the recently declared representative democracies provide privacy clauses among the individual rights enshrined in their constitutions. Some statements go so far as to detail what sorts of information an individual should expect government to protect and what should never be made public.

For example, Article 22 of the Lithuanian Constitution provides:

> The private life of an individual shall be inviolable. Personal correspondence, telephone conversation, telegraph message and other intercommunications shall be inviolable. Information concerning the private life of an individual may be collected only upon a justified court order and in accordance with the law. The law and the court shall protect individuals from arbitrary or unlawful interference in their private or family life, and from encroachment upon their honor and dignity.

These protections are clearly for the benefit of individuals and guard against intrusion from the public and government. The companion Law on Provision of Information to the Public not only reiterates a right of privacy[69] but also details what information is not to be provided to information distributors and what may not be published. The right of privacy protection states that "a person's right to have his personal and family life respected must be ensured… published only with the consent of that person [exceptions noted later in this law] and if the publication of such information does not cause undue harm to the person."

The only exceptions are when revelations of lawbreaking are the subject of publication; further, in the case of public figures, some case law suggests when the person's private life or personal traits are of public significance. The general prohibitions of what may be published, again according to some case law, include information that incites war, national, racial, religious, social, and gender hatred, that is slanderous and offensive to a person, or degrades human dignity and honor. Almost universally, the individual receives priority and protection from public scrutiny.

Many scholars have been concerned with the conflicts between a person's right to be left alone and the need for government to know about its citizens through data collection, distribution, and analysis.[70] Notification laws in the United States are a case in point for the conflicting values and the heated debate that they prompt. Wayne Logan provided a thorough examination of criminal registration and community notification laws in 2009. He wrote: "When the government singles out individuals in the interest of public safety, the message is clear: the individuals pose criminal risk and warrant fear. Under such circumstances, risk assessments are very material and notwithstanding any disclaimer."[71] But he wonders when society needs to consider the risks to privacy for those around the registrant.

> The social detriments can outweigh the benefits. This is because, today, more than ever before, a criminal conviction—especially involving a sex offender—serves as a perpetual badge of dishonor. The huge volume of daily "hits" recorded by Internet website registries make abundantly clear that something more than neutral information is being supplied and that the information is not being used by locals merely for self-protection.[72]

The innocents he worries about from this overuse of public information are the family members of registrants, employers, those who are mistakenly identified, and also the property values in neighborhoods where registrants or their families live. He voices the concern that the openness of the registration files becomes a directory for those who would use or abuse those who are registrants, targeting them for solicitations to buy or sell that which they are prohibited from having, or that they may become targets of those who are angry.

Government abuse of private information that is either mishandled or routinely made public has also been the subject of repeated inquiries from groups such as the American Civil Liberties Union and the Electronic Frontier Foundation, as well as journalists.[73] Perhaps there is currently no more constant conflict in the United States than that over access to email records of public officials who are either doing public work as if it were private or using public resources as if they were private. FOI requests are often the legal tool used for discovery, but very often the contents are sought because of concern about government bureaucrats using government email facilities for personal correspondence. Courts are increasingly using *in camera* review as a means of separating personal and "official business" email stored on government office servers.[74]

An early effort in the United States to sort out the handling of government documents was the promulgation of the Housekeeping Statute of 1789.[75] Among the instructions in the statute is one directed toward the executive branch.

> The said Secretary shall forthwith after his appointment be entitled to have the custody and charge of...all books, records and papers, remaining in the office of the last Secretary of the United States in Congress assembled; and such of the said books,

> records and papers, as may appertain to the Treasury department, or War department, shall be delivered over to the principal officers in the said department respectively, as the President of the United States shall direct.[76]

Tension in Congress concerning who controlled the information gathered and housed by the president and cabinet members and the executive branch existed from the organization of the government. As those offices went about their business, details of process or discussion were often the subject of speculation and curiosity. Though the Constitution required the president to provide reports "from time to time,"[77] there were some who thought there should be less time between reports.

Before the end of 1792, during George Washington's first administration, Congress launched an investigation into the decisions that were made by his cabinet that had ultimately led to the 1791 military defeat at the hands of the Wabash Indians. Congress requested all papers and records as part of its attempt to understand what had happened.[78] Washington was not inclined to release any of the internal notes and reports from his cabinet members, but when he conferred with Secretary of State Thomas Jefferson, he was told that the "executive ought to communicate such papers as the public good would permit, and ought to refuse those, the disclosure of which would injure the public…to exercise discretion."[79]

The discretion of the executive branch, now called executive privilege, was tested again within two years most pointedly with regard to Jay's Treaty. There were many questions about how the trade agreement described in the document had been arranged, and eventually the executive branch did provide some details.[80] Anger on the part of citizens was so fierce that Washington published his defense in newspapers as well as before Congress.[81]

President John Adams was the next one to feel the public sting during the controversial "XYZ Affair" of 1798. During the transatlantic negotiations with France, Adams encrypted his correspondence and did not produce these messages or the code when Congress asked for supporting materials before giving approval to prepare for another war. There was some suspicion that the coded messages did not shore up his case, so Adams finally supplied them. He asked that their contents be considered "confidential" and that Congress be mindful of the "consequences of their publication."[82]

This desire on the part of the executive branch to withhold deliberative information did not improve with Thomas Jefferson, the next president. He not only used codes for some correspondence but also kept parallel sets of letters for his personal files, and he was reported to have kept some of his presidential work "private" or "confidential" from congressional review.[83] Congress may not have pressed Jefferson very hard for reports and correspondence, but the courts were less forgiving. During the trial of Aaron Burr, Chief Justice John Marshall subpoenaed state papers. Jefferson insisted that though he was complying with the court's request for information, he would not appear personally at the hearing.[84] Justice Marshall did allow Jefferson to withhold some confidential information from the court as long as Marshall was sure no injustice would result.[85]

Nearly all presidents have claimed executive privilege, and some have extended that privilege to all of their cabinets. Often presidents issue a memo to their staff members about what is considered privileged and what must be available to the public.[86] For example, in the late twentieth century, President Ronald Reagan asserted a right of executive privilege and directed his cabinet staff in a memo to withhold information as each department thought prudent.[87] And presidents into the twenty-first century presumed privilege unless vigorously challenged by courts and congressional requests.

Congress wasn't much better about routinely pushing information toward constituents. Though both houses kept journals, any review of those journals was controlled. Even the members were somewhat frustrated by the superficiality of their contents. Connecticut resident Roger Sherman, one of only two colonials who served in both the Continental Congress and the Constitutional Convention and who also signed the Declaration of Independence, noted in a pamphlet: "I may, perhaps, be told, Congress do publish such a journal.... Has that journal ever been once laid before the General Assembly *officially* [Sherman's emphasis]...? If it has not, at whose door doth the neglect lie?"[88]

As the amount of information that government gathered and used began to pile up, the congresses of the twentieth century debated and then passed the Administrative Procedures Act to manage the storage of work documents and the procedures by which they could be accessed.[89] However, this exercise in moving information from executive and congressional offices to constituents often fell short, and legal scholars bemoaned the continued administrative stalling that often undermined what was intended as an enhancement to transparency.[90] Efforts were made to encourage citizen engagement by enacting the 1966 Freedom of Information Act,[91] and by establishing in 1962 the Depository Library System[92] in every voting district. However, public notice remained the sole legal requirement that government actually routinely post in public newspapers information about government activities that would directly affect individuals. For centuries, newspapers were the vehicle of choice for distributing this sort of information—both the formal public notices often seen as boxed advertisements and the less formal news reports that journalists picked up from legislative journals and executive branch reports.[93]

Emails and work papers aside, the issue of private versus public information dissemination prompted one writer to suggest that legislatures definitively state that all work products are part of the public record: "The trend [of excluding personal emails from the scope of state public records statutes] threatens to undermine the strong presumption in favor of public access…and hinder public access to government email records that may reveal official misconduct."[94] As the debate over email in particular continues to rage into the early twenty-first century, our focus here will be on public information that is government held and has already gone through the legal machinations of separating private from public to determine what must be protected from public access and distribution. If we look to other representative democracies, we can see some commonalities in the reasons given for wide distribution of public information.

Public Information Values

As far back as the early Greek city-states, the governments of working democracies recognized the value of public access to government records as a means of keeping bureaucrats accountable for their activities, but they also understood the value of public records as a way to educate the public through authentic or official text. These sometimes competing interests of accountability and authenticity get in the way of the needs of both the government and the public in endorsing these sorts of records. The use of records, history seems to show us, may affect a society's perception of how government-held information should be made available.

For example, laws within a Greek city-state, which were sometimes shared among neighbors, promoted peaceful coexistence when some sort of official record could be referenced for everyone's use. The earliest records among the Greek states seem to concern primarily magistrates' activities. These reports detailed their decisions in the day-to-day duties they were asked to perform. As early as the seventh century B.C.E., these reports or records helped maintain consistency as the magistrate duties passed among members of the state,[95] and it is not difficult to imagine how these records became important across generations. Inventories of treasures and goods housed in sacred buildings and accounts of public funds and expenditures were also records that were kept in a formal, fixed format for use across time.[96]

Records of public stores and daily decisions kept by magistrates were not the only kind of documents created and kept for public use. Literacy was so high among the Athenians by the third century B.C.E. that classic texts were being copied at high rates. Occasionally the copyists were careless, and errors increasingly cropped up in these socially important texts.[97]

During the period of Lycurgus, 338–325 B.C.E., a law required that written versions of the tragedies of Aeschylus, Sophocles, and Euripides be held in the city's records office. The clerk was also required to read and know these official versions of text so well that he could compare them to the versions presented by actors. Actors who were found to deviate from the authentic versions were punished.[98] These official versions were thought to be so authentic and important that when the Ptolemys were establishing their Alexandria library, they acquired all of these texts from Athens rather than accept copies.[99]

Though the library at Alexandria was not a government "records office," it did serve as a major public library.[100] Ptolemy I opened it for unrestricted use by all who were literate and by anyone interested in authoritative versions of records and reports. Several generations of Ptolemys collected the original of every written text from every ship docked in Alexandria and every nation that the Ptolemys ruled, making that library collection a vast array of documents including everything literary, scholarly, and legal.[101]

The practice of document collecting and the distinction of authentic books and documents stayed with leadership around the world. Many centuries later, some of the framers of the U.S. Constitution maintained large collections of books and papers. Some of their personal libraries became the core collections for public libraries.[102] Among the better known of these collections was that of Thomas Jefferson, who sold his library of more than 6,000 volumes to the young U.S. Congress so that the government would have a collection for reference.[103]

The value of a public repository was not lost on the framers of the U.S. Constitution. As noted in Chapter 1 of this work, Article I, §5, of the U.S. Constitution, as well as clauses in various state constitutions,[104] required that an official record or a journal of activities be kept and made public. The Massachusetts constitution offered this rationale for public documents: "The people…have a right to require of their lawgivers and magistrates an exact and constant observation of them, in the formation and execution of the laws necessary for the good administration of the commonwealth."[105]

Accessibility as a Value of Public Information

From the establishment of the U.S. Library of Congress soon after the first congressional session closed in 1791, librarians were important not only in safeguarding access to government-held information, but also in prodding government to be as forthcoming as the law would permit with "popular information."[106]

Government documents librarians have often served as the watchdogs for use and accessibility of those records in their charge.[107] In retrospect, their efforts may sometimes seem over-zealous, unless one takes into account the social standards of the early federation. One little-known practice of the eighteenth-century U.S. Senate was to close its sessions to the public. Journals of proceedings were kept, as mandated by the Constitution, and were available for inspection. But the details of debate, who voted on which side of each issue, and any of the deliberations affecting a bill's passage or failure were not part of the public records. In fact, visitors were barred from the floor of the Senate for the first three sessions.[108]

Authenticity as a Value of Public Information

As copies were made, the Greeks were concerned about consistency in the records, and they established a mechanism for ensuring fidelity to the original text. That same concern is evident today as records move from mechanical duplication to transformation in format. The changing environment of government-held information from paper format to digital archive has spawned concerns from every group of stakeholders. Among the issues raised is that of authentication for public records distributed on the Internet.[109]

An important aspect of authenticity is a concern about the legitimacy of records. Many a mystery has turned on the telltale characteristic of paper documents that allows readers to notice if text has been altered or pages are missing. In the digital world there is no easily accessible comparison for sleuthing. How can those who search the web for government documents know that what is before them is what it claims to be? The concern about authenticity, which exists today much as it did in Athens centuries ago, suggests that it is a deeply rooted value that we expect government to address.

The issue of authenticity certainly has proven to be a modern-day impediment for government's efforts at efficiency. The trend of outsourcing record handling with companies who actually do the work of data generation, collection, storage, and retrieval is both boon and bane. A survey of U.S. state-level practices in 2000 reported that government records were increasingly generated and held by private individuals who, in turn, were responsible for public access to them. The review found that the available websites were at best uneven.[110] Some of these state-level government entities, it was observed, managed the private sector's contribution across all agencies under a single set of rules, while others either relied on the courts or on case-by-case decisions to develop and employ access guidelines.

Ownership as a Value of Public Information

Government documents that seem to have shifting or undefined ownership pose another concern. When, for example, does government-held information, such as the private papers of those who were in public office, become public information? The issue has been with the American system since its first government, and has most often played out when presidents want to control some portion of their work output. Sometimes the conflict has arisen when executive branch letters or memos are sought by Congress, or when collectors want a memento for private use.

A prime early example of this controversy involved George Washington's nephew, Bushrod Washington, who gave his uncle's papers to any and all who asked for them. Several of the early presidents transferred ownership of their personal work papers to family heirs.[111] Some presidents ordered that their papers be destroyed. Sometimes presidents transferred ownership to nonfamily members outside of government purview.[112] This all suggests that there was at least some belief that presidential work papers belonged to the man in the office. Franklin Roosevelt was among the presidents who donated their papers to a library established for the purpose of housing presidential work papers. In Roosevelt's case, he was explicit in his expectation that those works would be available to the public.[113]

Though Roosevelt's donation of his work papers appeared to be a gift rather than the fulfillment of a legal obligation, his action suggests some change in attitude by public officeholders.[114] Some scholars have suggested that modern U.S. disputes are more about shifting interpretations of the intentions of the Constitution's framers than the specifics of more general property rights theory.[115] Returning to Lithuania as an example, the law there requires that "[s]tate and municipal institutions and agencies must inform the public of their activities."[116] The law further requires that "private information available to the said institutions, except for cases specified in the law where private information is not to be divulged," is to be public. Since the accompanying law, as mentioned earlier in this chapter, specifically allows public figures' private lives to be subject to public review, it is logical to infer that work papers may well be public information by law in that country.[117]

The social values of public information, it seems, shape the contours of private information when it becomes part of government-held resources. Those values include accessibility to government activities and knowing what government is doing, public sharing in official or legitimate accounts of government reports, and the community ownership in those reports and documents. It is this communal value that supports conversation, examination, suggestion, rebuttal, and shared experience, and makes representative democracies function even in times of stress and extreme discord. What are the conditions that require government to go another step? Why and when is government required not only to gather, keep, and make available this public store of information, but also to actively inform community members that particular items in this data reservoir need attention?

Public Notice and Government

A social value of public notice is that everyone, equally, can know about something of importance to the party posting the notice. There are many examples of private businesses or individuals placing notices in newspapers and other public venues so as to make clear some particular subject matter. It can be as simple as a going-out-of-business sale or as complicated as the desire to distinguish one person from another. In the first example, the business wants the most attention it can get for its final sale. In the second example, the posting party wants to be sure that another person's debts or legal complications are not confused with the good standing of the person who posted the notice. While these examples are not public notices required by law, the declaration of the display ad proclaiming it a public notice is clearly an effort to get attention and provide some positive proof of action.

When government is the party posting a public notice, the intentions are somewhat the same. The public notice serves to get the most attention possible for the business of government, and, by keeping all members informed with official facts and figures, society has the best chance of group-sourcing bright ideas. Viewed in this way, public notice becomes central to the success of a representative democracy.

This chapter has primarily identified public notice in terms of written documents, but there are some scholars who look to any kind of government decree in whatever form as part of the history of public notice. Charles Allen, in his *Series of Articles on Public Notice*, traced the origins of public notice to oral traditions, when town criers or those who could read reported verbatim what was said or written by those in authority.[118] The intention of the oral communication was to distribute the decrees of kings, for example, to all the population quickly and with at least some degree of accuracy.

This kind of relay system has its drawbacks, of course. The messenger must keep the message simple, and the listener must be able to recall any necessary details. It also requires that the messenger and listener be in proximity to one another at the time of the message delivery—a messenger-centric system. A public notice system like this requires that the listener get to the messenger in good time, rather than the other way around, where the messenger just waits patiently for the attention of the listener.

Another means of distributing public information was by posting a notice in some sort of fixed format, physically, in a high-traffic area. The Greek city-states and the Roman Empire used this method, and some cultures in the Americas similarly employed drawings on rocks or paintings on fabrics. Even in the twenty-first century, in cases where social structures are under pressure, governments still use a printed notice posted on trees or in town squares as a way of getting information to its citizens.[119] This method of providing information to a community had the benefit of consistency—everyone who could read saw exactly the same notice—and there was less concern about having missed the message because it could remain posted for any amount of time.

In an autocracy, the messenger or town crier for public notice might be effective enough. The purpose of the public notice is simply to tell the population what is expected of it or to impart important news that the citizens had better heed. But in a representative democracy, government information is not just about bulletins or alerts. This form of government requires putting the best ideas to work in any given situation, and, historically, it is evident that good ideas can come from almost any corner of a nation.

Governments have found public notice to be a good venue for all sorts of work. A 2010 law journal article outlined the uses that government has for public notice today. Public notices solicit purchasing bids, announce licensing, and facilitate property reclamation.[120] Notices are also a means of alerting everyone about pending litigation, changes in the law, and plans for government activity. In some cases public notices are used to reach the nearly unreachable—individuals who have some sort of pending business with government but for whom no viable address can be located. In each of these instances of public notice, the desire of government is to reach out to the citizenry rather than require that community members seek out information about government activities. Though there are some similarities in function, each of these uses of public notice and the desired outcomes are slightly different. A brief look at the various kinds of public notice applications follows.

Government Information and Public Notice Outcomes

When government is interested in efficiently purchasing goods and services, it is often required to post a public notice soliciting bids, a procedure that assures that everyone is given equal opportunity to respond. It also provides the opportunity for public inspection before commitment to purchase is made. The entire process has several benefits. Everyone who wants to participate knows what is asked of the bidders and what the government needs. Those who want to inspect also have the opportunity to know what was requested and how much the government will be paying for the goods or services.

The public notice procedure for property reclamation is slightly different. In this case the government is declaring certain overriding social needs and the avenue of satisfying those needs. Notice is simply a way of alerting the community to a certain set of actions and what may soon transpire. The decision about taking property and repurposing it has already been made, and the time for action is very near. Similarly, public notice of licensing awards is another straight-up announcement. These postings are a way of informing the community about who may practice what sort of specialty, but the time for challenges is past, and the notice is more of a public note. In addition, public notices about changes in the law are an instance of simply informing everyone that something new has been added or taken away from the regulations that guide good citizenship. While the time for contesting or challenging the rationale for change is past, law-abiding citizens would want to be kept abreast of new laws. All of these are examples of government merely keeping the electorate informed about government works already enacted.

An entirely different set of public notice actions are meant to elicit community involvement at the most opportune moment for input. These would include pending litigation, government's planning activities, and the routine reporting of treasurers' offices, zoning boards, and development offices. The purpose of these notices is to inform the public but also to give community members the opportunity to participate as things progress. These public notices may be as simple as postings of meeting agendas or as complicated as full-budget reports. In all of these cases, the public notices are often routine and scheduled so that the public knows when to look and where. In short, the public gets used to noticing these items and may choose to ignore them, but expects them nonetheless.

In some cases public notices are used as a last resort when direct contact of an individual becomes nearly impossible. Almost every representative democracy expects its government to make an effort to find those who will be affected by impending action. Draft board notices and foreclosure notices require that every effort be made to locate persons and serve them with registered documents. But there are times when a person's whereabouts are unknown. Public notice is the venue when all others fail. The intention in this case is that the affected person will either, by chance, see the notice displayed in a public place, or some member of the public will see the notice and inform the individual that his or her attention is required. While often disparaged as ineffective, public notice in these situations is understood to rank a poor second to constructive notice, but it is sometimes the only choice available.

Clearly, the intention of public notices is not uniform, and various kinds of notices serve different social purposes. So it might be expected that as societies reflect on their uses and norms, there would be different codes for these several situations. The next chapters will discuss in more detail the modern language used to describe when and how public notice is employed, and will provide a range of examples of social constructs for them.

· 3 ·

MODERN LEGAL DEFINITIONS OF PUBLIC NOTICE

Public notice as a social concept has been with us for centuries, but public notice as defined in law, sometimes referred to as legal notice or legal advertising, has had a somewhat shorter history. This chapter will highlight some of the principles and uses of public notice as a legal construct.

Many of the early uses by government of public notice come through common law case notes.[121] As John Rayner noted in his thorough work on libel laws of England, "Common law is common reason…not thereby that common reason wherewith a man is naturally endued, but that perfection of reason which is gotten by long and continual study."[122] Among the eighteenth-century references to public notice is a complaint about newspapers disseminating misinformation in the name of authority.[123] But perhaps more important was the legal assertion that government should keep public records, and that they would be available for inspection for any reason at all.[124]

The legal assertion in these cases is that the government should, of course, keep records, and that those records should be available to anyone who needs to consult them. But these court opinions do not assert that it is the responsibility of the government to bring those records to the attention of anyone who might be affected by what the documents contain. That notion of providing information directly to the citizens, as a legal requirement of the community, is in scant evidence in the period before colonial America became the United States.

An early American codification of public notice can be found in the first session of the first U.S. Congress, when the legislature required that the Secretary of State keep a record of all legislative activity and that

> Every such law, order, resolution and vote…be published in at least three of the public newspapers printed within the United States, and…one printed copy…delivered to each Senator and Representative of the United States, and two printed copies duly authenticated to be sent to the Executive authority of each State….[125]

The newly established government was concerned, no doubt, about making sure that its rules and orders were not only taken seriously but were considered the law of the land. By posting them throughout the young country, there would certainly be more confidence that the work of Congress would be evident. Eventually the *Congressional Record*, available in every voting district through a network of depository libraries, became the publication of record. Whatever it was called, the wide distribution of reports, votes, and activities became a public record that was made available to everyone and as close to home as possible.

Promulgation of legislative activity was not the only subject for public notice, however, as the executive branch and courts were also concerned with getting the word out about new rules or adjudication. Eventually the executive branch would provide daily logs that are now known as the *Federal Register* and the weekly publication of the presidency known as the *Weekly Compilation of Presidential Documents*. The courts publish their opinions in a variety of subscriber compilations, but officially they are carried in the *Federal Reporter* for trial and appellate courts, and the *United States Reports* for the Supreme Court. All of these became staples of the depository library system that now includes about a thousand locations across the United States.

The specifics of public notice have received renewed interest as communication environments have changed from primarily paper-based formats to digital platforms. In a popular text of the twentieth century, concerns were raised about the veracity of entire areas of the law when documents were vulnerable to morphing and disappearance, copyright infringement, and electronic subterfuge, all of which were prevalent for a time.[126] But attention to other aspects of public notice, such as cost, visibility, and distribution, were voiced repeatedly.[127] At the dawn of the twenty-first century, U.S. state legislatures began seriously tinkering with the details of public notice law. Dozens of states either began allowing summaries of previously required full-length documents and reports, or providing that full notices be posted online rather than in previously established newspapers of record.[128]

As societies have become less worried about the risks involved, and with assurances of digital preparation, presentation, archiving, and management, the fears surrounding electronic formats have abated. Often, however, the details of the laws that describe public notice requirements have not kept up.

For example, between the years 2006 and 2007, a review of U.S. state laws requiring public notice publication found that they varied significantly. The only generalization that could be made about the range of changes was that the requirements were in flux.[129] The review found at least 167 legislative acts that changed state laws guiding public notice during that period, and nearly two dozen court cases examining the case law around public notice requirements.

Four years later, the states were still wrestling with the definition of legal or public notice. In 2011 alone at least 19 states enacted laws clarifying what constituted public or legal notice.[130] Evidently the special features of public notice matter a great deal to particular communities, and some of those details will be examined here.

Evolving Definitions of Public Notice

Gilbert Bailey, in his 1941 *Legal Advertising*, written primarily for news organizations, summarized public notice this way:

> The term…comprises three kinds of legal notices: the promulgation of laws, the service of process by publication, and public advertising, which are respectively intended to protect the individual against the unnotified exercise of legislative, judicial or executive power by enforcing his right to know: (1) what the law is, (2) when his interests are to be judicially determined, (3) how the public business is conducted.[131]

This concise rendering of both the principle and values of the public notice is useful for the more complete review of legal applications of the concept. Early uses of public notice, as already mentioned, were most often about keeping text error-free, as with the Greek historical plays. Other uses included proclamations from government to help citizens stay abreast of the law or conform to government edicts, such as census compilation. *Maine's Ancient Law* provides reference to early legal requirements met by public notice as a way of holding citizens accountable for observing the law.[132] Codes literally chiseled in stone and put in public places were undeniable reminders of what constituted acceptable behavior. The Twelve Tables,[133] for example, became a standard for all new laws and litigation about old understandings during the thousand years of Roman political dominance spanning most of Europe and the Mediterranean region.[134]

Publication as a means of providing public notice is not universal, as James Bryce noted in his 1901 *Studies in History and Jurisprudence*. He reports, for example, that in Iceland the law was recited aloud in a public forum at regular intervals by a community speaker, or declarer, who was also obliged to explain and interpret confusing provisions. In this way the community was put on notice about what constituted the laws of the land, and all members were expected to adhere to the orders henceforth.[135]

As governments became more sensitive to the effectiveness of administration, it became evident that the citizenry responded more enthusiastically when informed in advance of new rules enacted. It is important to note how, as England's 1215 Magna Carta was refined by subsequent confirmations and pronouncements, the laws were believed to be more enforceable when the public was adequately informed by written texts at regular intervals. For example, in 1297 King Edward I announced that it would be required that "charters [laws] shall be sent under our seal to cathedral churches throughout our realm, and there remain, and shall be read before the people twice in the year."[136]

The local housing of the laws continued for centuries among the English, though the locations changed as the monarchy distanced itself from the Catholic faith. By the reign of King Henry VII in the late fifteenth century, it was the practice of leadership to send transcripts of all the current court session's acts to each sheriff of the county seats. A writ would command the sheriff to "cause those statutes and all articles contained to be publicly proclaimed and strictly obeyed, and kept in every place where it should seem expedient."[137]

As printing presses became more readily available, it also became easier to print multiple copies of the laws as they were written and for those copies to be widely distributed. Publication and distribution with local authorities became the new standard, since the expectation was already in place that the law wasn't really the law until the general public was informed of it.[138] The guidelines for publication were prescribed in detail within English law as early as the thirteenth century, so noted in the *Statutes of the Realm*. And it became primarily the job of members of Parliament to be sure that the laws were made known to the rank and file of their respective counties.[139]

As the laws of any land became more complicated, the kinds of content became more specialized. The areas of law that most often require public notice now include many things—not only legislative acts, but executive orders, administrative rules, and judicial decisions. A recent sampling from the *Times of India* found public notices of the qualifications for those hired as university lecturers and assistant professors, the completion date for review of a government-sponsored urban master plan, and declarations of disowning children.[140]

Legal Definitions

The specifics of what constitutes public notice are not quite as simple as referring to an all-purpose glossary or even a law dictionary. *Black's Law Dictionary*, the standard for most Western, English-language legal systems, includes a lengthy entry for "notice" quoted here only in part.

> Notice may be either (1) statutory, i.e., made so by legislative enactment; (2) actual, which brings the knowledge of a fact directly home to the party; or (3) constructive. Constructive notice may be subdivided into: (a) Where there exists actual notice of matter, to which equity has added constructive notice of facts, which an inquiry after such matter would have elicited; and (b) where there has been a designed abstinence from inquiry for the very purpose of escaping notice.[141]

The entry goes on to detail "actual notice," "averment of notice," "express notice," "implied notice," "personal notice," and "public notice," defined as "Notice given to the public generally, or to the entire community, or to all whom it may concern. Such must commonly be published in a newspaper of general circulation."

The components of this definition merit some attention as well. Distribution to all concerned is an important concept associated with public notice, as is the expectation that some information, by virtue of its community interest, is expressly for public inspection and consumption. With as many variations of notice as *Black's Law Dictionary* presents, it is easy to understand that untangling the necessary aspects of any particular kind of notification is daunting.

Variations described in the laws pertaining to public notice among local jurisdictions in the United States, for example, include slightly different names for the concept. Public notice may be referred to as legal notice, official notice, or record notice. Publication may occur in newspapers that publish regularly and have a verified paid circulation at a certain level. Publication may also take place through web posting, post office or community building display, or by television broadcast. If notice is published in the newspaper, there are some states that require certain placement within the pages of that publication. Usually the text itself must be in English—though not always—and must be of a certain size type. Often there are requirements about how often a notice must be published or aired, posted, or replaced. And sometimes there are requirements about the timing of the publication, that is, so many days or weeks before or after an event of public interest.[142]

By the mid-nineteenth century, legal scholars were compiling more detailed reference materials to distinguish the many iterations of public notice in the United States. Here is a sample from William Wade's *A Treatise on the Law of Notice as Affecting Civil Rights and Remedies* provided in a single, very thick volume.

> §1029. General Character of Service by Publication. Publication is a means authorized by statute in most, if not all the states of the Union, for obtaining constructive service of process, when from the non-residence, absence from the state, or absconding of the defendant, a more direct mode of service becomes impracticable.
>
> Service of summons in this manner is called constructive, not because the publication in the manner prescribed by statute raises any reasonable presumption that thereby the defendant is advised of the pendency of the suit, for its authorization is not confined to cases where there is even a possibility of its ever coming to the knowledge of the party to be affected. The defendant may have removed so far beyond the confines of civilization that it would be impossible in the nature of things for the paper containing the first insertion of the notice to reach him before the return day, and it will still be as effective as though the paper came regularly to his hands.[143]
>
> §1030 Must Conform to Statute. As this manner of serving process depends for its validity more upon its strict conformity to the statue by which it is authorized than upon an inherent probability of its conveying intelligence of the impending suit to the party whose rights are to be affected, the fact that it has actually come to the knowledge of defendant cannot be shown to supply any material deviation in the publication from what the statute prescribes. The statute, being in derogation of common law, is always strictly construed and it must be shown affirmatively that its provisions have been complied with. (*Scorpion* S.M.Co. *v. Marsano*, 10 Nev., 370; *Likens v.* McCormick, 39 Wis. 313)[144]
>
> §1068 Substitute for Publication Paper. ...such as posting the notice in several public places within the county, but this method of publishing notices is so rarely employed for the purpose of obtaining service of process that it will not receive further notice.[145]
>
> §1080 Proof of Publication Next, as to the proof of publication, a compliance with the prerequisites of the statute with respect to publication is usually established by the affidavit of the printer or publisher of the paper in which the notice is published.

This, however, is a matter of statutory regulation, and in general is not prescribed to the exclusion of all other modes of proof.[146]

Almost a century later, a newer compilation was published in a three-volume set prepared by Maurice Merrill, citing case law and statutes as helpful details, and acknowledging that there were important differences among the several states and federal governments.

Vol. 1 §2 Analysis of Notice
The concept of notice includes:

Cognitive Notice: knowledge, facts putting one on inquiry, notification which need not be remembered;

Absolute notice: notification by formal communication, by performance as in recording instruments, notice by publication, notice by posting, notice by legislation, juristic formulation of legal rules, etc.;

Unforgettable knowledge: Facts which one is under a duty to know.[147]

Vol. 2 Chapter 16 Notification by Posting §694 In the Absence of Express Authorization

In the absence of express authorization, the great weight of authority holds that once does not effectively give notification by posting a document in even the most public of places.... Custom, at least of a private nature, cannot give any sanctity to the placard.[148]

Vol. 3 §1102 Introductory Note

The [case law] books abound with instances wherein pleas of ignorance concerning public acts are rejected and persons who never were aware of them are held to be affected thereby in their property and in their lives.[149]

Vol. 3 §1103 Principles of Common Law

"God forbid," Chief Justice Abbott piously said to a jury [in 1825], "that it should be imagined that an attorney, or a counsel, or even a judge is bound to know all the law..." (*Montriou v. Jeffreys*, 2 C&P 113, 172 Eng. Repr. 51 [1825]).

Yet the aphorism that everyone "is charged with knowledge of the law" remains popular as a judicial summing up of the reasons why in particular cases a man is not permitted to evade the legal consequences attaching to his action or inaction by the pleas that he did not know them. (State e rel. *Hatfield v. Moreland*, 152 Okl. 37, 3 P2d 803 (1931).[150]

Each of the elements described here speaks only to *how* the notice will be made public. As to the *content* of public notices, there are literally thousands of requirements about what must be made public within U.S. jurisdictions, and equally so in many other representative democracies. Here are just a few examples.

From New Zealand, the New Zealand Herald:

> "NOTICE OF INTENTION TO REMOVE COMPANY FROM REGISTER MATERIALS LIMITED (IN LIQUIDATION) the Company Pursuant to section 320 of the Companies Act 1993 (the Act) (a) It is intended that the above named company be removed from the New Zealand Register under Section 318(1)(e) of the Act, on the grounds that the duties of the liquidator have been completed and the liquidator has sent to the Registrar the documents referred to in Section 257(1)(a) of the Act. (b) Any objection to the removal under Section 321 of the Act must be lodged with the Registrar together with the grounds for such objection no later than 21 March 2013. Note: This is a solvent liquidation and the liquidation is a result of the restructuring of the company's business affairs by the shareholders. VICTORIA TOON LIQUIDATOR Dated at Auckland this 15th February 2013 C/- Corporate Restructuring Limited Chartered Accountants Level 12, 17 Albert Street AUCKLAND 1010 P O Box 10100 Dominion Road AUCKLAND 1446, Published Monday, February 18, 2013, First Published Monday, February 18, 2013

From Switzerland:

> http://www.ictregulationtoolkit.org/en/Publication.766.html, Public invitation to tender for radio licenses for the provision of telecommunications services based on the GSM standard in Switzerland
> Published July 2003, viewed February 2013.

From the International Monetary Fund in compliance with Germany's public notice laws:

> "IMF Executive Board Concludes 2012 Article IV Consultation with Germany, Public Information Notice (PIN) No. 12/69July 3, 2012, Public Information Notices (PINs) form part of the IMF's efforts to promote transparency of the IMF's views and analysis of economic developments and policies. With the consent of the country (or countries) concerned, PINs are issued after Executive Board discussions of Article IV consultations with member countries, of its

surveillance of developments at the regional level, of post-program monitoring, and of ex post assessments of member countries with longer-term program engagements. PINs are also issued after Executive Board discussions of general policy matters, unless otherwise decided by the Executive Board in a particular case. The staff report for the 2012 Article IV Consultation with Germany is also available. On June 29, 2012, the Executive Board of the International Monetary Fund (IMF) concluded the Article IV consultation with Germany."
http://www.imf.org/external/np/sec/pn/2012/pn1269.htm, viewed February 2013.

From Iceland, Air Atlantic Iceland:

LEGAL NOTICE Agreement to Terms of Use
These Terms and Conditions of Use (the "Terms of Use") apply to the Air Atlanta Icelandic (collectively "AAI") web site located at www.airatlanta.com, and all associated sites linked to www.airatlanta.com by AAI, its subsidiaries and affiliates, including AAI subsidiary sites around the world (collectively, the "Site"). The Site is the property of AAI and its licensors. BY USING THE SITE, YOU AGREE TO THESE TERMS OF USE; IF YOU DO NOT AGREE, DO NOT USE THE SITE.
http://www.atlanta.is/index.aspx?GroupId=50, viewed February 2013

From Finland, the United Kingdom, and the United States:

Federal Register Public Notice on Adding Finland and United Kingdom as Reciprocating Nations, DCL-08–46, December 10, 2008
Information About: State/Local Child Support Agencies
Topics: Intergovernmental/Interstate, International
Types: Policy, Dear Colleague Letters (DCL)
Tags: Foreign Reciprocating Countries (FRC)
DEAR COLLEAGUE LETTER, DCL-08–46
DATE: Dec 10, 2008
RE: Additional Reciprocating Nations
Dear Colleague: In DCL-08–10, issued on March 26, 2008, OCSE announced that Finland and the United Kingdom had each been declared a "foreign reciprocating country" or FRC for child support enforcement purposes by the United States pursuant to 42 U.S.C. 659A authority. On November 28, 2008, the Office of the Legal Adviser, U.S. Department of State, published the enclosed cumulative public notice on completed Federal reciprocity declarations in the Federal Register (73 FR 72555). You may find this Federal Register notice useful in proceedings where the existence of a reciprocal relationship is at issue.
http://www.acf.hhs.gov/programs/css/resource/fr-notice-on-adding-finland-and-united-kingdom-as-reciprocating-nations, viewed February 2013

From Malta's Environment and Planning Authority:

L.N. 52 of 2013 ENVIRONMENT AND DEVELOPMENT PLANNING ACT (CAP. 504) Environment and Development Planning Act (Amendment of Eighth Schedule) Regulations, 2013 BY VIRTUE of the powers conferred by articles 61(2)(q) and 62 of the Environment and Development Planning Act, the Minister for Tourism, Culture and the Environment, after consultation with the Malta Environment and Planning Authority, has made the following regulations:
1. (1) The title of these regulations is the Environment and Development Planning Act (Amendment of Eighth Schedule) Regulations, 2013, and these regulations shall be read and construed as one with the Eighth Schedule of the Environment and Development Planning Act, hereinafter referred to as "the Eighth Schedule". (2) These regulations shall come into force as follows: (a) with respect to developments within residences within areas zoned for terraced development in the development zone specified in sub-categories (i), (ii), (iii) and (iv) of paragraph 1 of Category B, as substituted by regulation 2, these regulations shall be deemed to have come into force on 1st August, 2012; and (b) with respect to all other developments specified in the remaining sub-categories of paragraph 1 of Category B, as substituted by regulation 2, these regulations shall come into force on 29th January, 2013. Published January 29, 2013." http://www.mepa.org.mt/, viewed February 2013

From Australia, Fairfax Media:

Saturday February 16, 2013, The Sydney Morning Herald
AGNEW, Beverley Vera, 14.7.1923–14.2.2013
Late of Paddington, formerly of Tasmania.
Much loved sister of Stewart (dec), Nancye (dec), Del (dec), Lucy (dec), Eric and their families. Family and friends are warmly invited to attend BEVS Funeral Service to be held in the Camellia Chapel, Macquarie Park Crematorium, cnr Delhi & Plassey Rds, North Ryde on Thursday (21 February, 2013) at 12.30 pm. By request no flowers.
ALBERT & MEYER, AUSTRALIAN OWNED, Thornleigh 9484 3992
FDA of NSW

From Nepal:

Source Nepal Gazette 2008 Notice Of Government Of Nepal Posted on February 18th, 2013 12:00:35 PM
Notice-1 Source A) Wage rate and working hour determination
Notice-1 Source: Nepal Gazette (2008), Notice of Government of Nepal (GoN), Ministry of Labour and Transport, Part 58, Supplementary 25 (e), Department of Print, [Filename: Nepal Gazette (2009) Notices 201 20 and 202 Minimum wage for agriculture and all other enterprises.pdf]
http://docsfiles.com/pdf_source_nepal_gazette_2008_notice_of_government_of_nepal.html, viewed February 2013

This small sample supports the generalization that public notice is nearly universal among many variations of representative governments, and concerns many areas of public life. The above examples range from business liquidation to hourly wage rates, from individual death notices to international collection of child support, and from national environmental protections to national airline services.

The Public Notice Umbrella

Modern-day laws requiring that the public be made aware of government activity concern notice of law-making or law-changing (legislatures), notice of administrative processes or proceedings (courts and enforcement), and notice of the conduct of government business (executive branch).

In turn, then, law-making is defined as anything having to do with the enacted statute—all the way back through the process of information collection—that affects the decision making around a law's specific language, as well as the subsequent information that affects voting on particular measures, and then ultimately promulgation of laws. In some communities this even includes court decisions that affect understanding of the law.

Administrative processes that require or encourage the use of public notice are usually those aligned with courts and law enforcement. When officers of the court are directed to process complaints or serve notice, every representative democracy expects ample means of knowing what has transpired to engage the courts' activities upon individual members of that society.

Executive branch activities also include deliberations, budgets, hiring of staff, planning, and deploying community projects. In many cases this includes purchasing, setting utility rates, collecting fees, community planning, and implementing improvements, as well as assisting in community recovery from disasters.

Public notice serves community needs in a variety of ways. In order for representative democracies to work effectively and efficiently, there needs to be a set of standards in place, accepted by all members to ensure that the information contained in any public notice is accurate, correctly contextualized, timely, and authentic. In short, public notice needs to carry a certain amount of authority for everyone to respect the value of the notification.

In the course of many centuries, certain kinds of systems have developed to assure the validity of public notices. A bond of trust in the sequence of creating, processing, and presenting public notices meant that when a citizen was served papers from the court, or committee reports were published, or budgets were posted, the questions from constituents weren't about the process but about the content. What was being asked by the court? What did the report say? What will the budget require in taxes? As societies move into a digital world for communicating messages that relies on the abstractions of zeros and ones, conduits and massive data warehouses, the transparency of the old systems is vanishing.

Legal Expressions of Public Notice

What follows is a somewhat detailed account of how the law has evolved in its use, serving the segregated interests suggested in the first part of this chapter—legislative, judicial, and executive branches of government. Sometimes the laws surrounding public notice are intended for a specific situation or condition of social life, and sometimes the public notice laws overarch an entire aspect of society. This selection will capture the range of legal expressions for public notice, as well as provide a context for the examples of modern public notice use provided in the next chapter.

Constitutional, Statutory, and Administrative Statements

In the United States, the laws directing public notice can be found at every level of government. The general directive, already noted in Chapter 2 of this book, was part of the first session of Congress in 1789. Since then every agency has requirements as part of its core documents, directing the kinds of information that must be posted. Some examples include requirements during the patent process, federal communications licensing process, transportation, and water pollution controls. Here is the specific language of those regulations:

> Licensing federally owned inventions [requirements]...
> (e) Public notice. No exclusive or partially exclusive license may be granted under section 207(a)(2) [35 USCS §207(a)(2)] unless public notice of the intention to grant an exclusive or partially exclusive license on a federally owned invention has been provided in an appropriate manner at least 15 days before the license is granted, and the Federal agency has considered all comments received before the end of the comment period in response to that public notice. This subsection shall not apply to the licensing of inventions made under a cooperative research and development agreement entered into under section 12 of the Stevenson-Wydler Technology Innovation Act of 1980 (15 U.S.C. 3710a).[151]

Universal Service Procedures…
(5) Requirements for certain schools with computers having Internet access.
(iii) Public notice; hearing. An elementary or secondary school described in clause (i), or the school board, local educational agency, or other authority with responsibility for administration of the school, shall provide reasonable public notice and hold at least 1 public hearing or meeting to address the proposed Internet safety policy. In the case of an elementary or secondary school other than an elementary or secondary school as defined in section 14101 of the Elementary and Secondary Education Act of 1965 (20 U.S.C. 8801), the notice and hearing required by this clause may be limited to those members of the public with a relationship to the school.[152]

Enforcement of Water Pollution Prevention…
(2) Whenever, on the basis of information available to him, the Administrator finds that violations of permit conditions or limitations as set forth in paragraph (1) of this subsection are so widespread that such violations appear to result from a failure of the State to enforce such permit conditions or limitations effectively, he shall so notify the State. If the Administrator finds such failure extends beyond the thirtieth day after such notice, he shall give public notice of such finding….[153]
Motor Vehicle Safety Notification Procedures….
(3) In addition to the notification required under paragraphs (1) and (2), if the Secretary decides that public notice is required for motor vehicle safety, public notice shall be given by the manufacturer in the way required by the Secretary after consulting with the manufacturer. In deciding whether public notice is required, the Secretary shall consider–
(A) the magnitude of the risk to motor vehicle safety caused by the defect or noncompliance; and
(B) the cost of public notice compared to the additional number of owners the notice may reach.

(4) A dealer to whom a motor vehicle or replacement equipment was delivered shall be notified in the manner prescribed by the Secretary, by regulation.[154]

New Zealand has a general statutory guide to public notice with a short title as follows:

An Act—(a) to provide for the printing and publication of copies of Acts of Parliament and statutory regulations; and (b) to ensure that copies of Acts of Parliament and statutory regulations are available to the public; and (c) to provide for the Government Printing Office to cease to be a department of the Public Service.

The act goes on to say in Section 4 of Public Act No. 142 of 1989 that:

Under the Acts and Regulations Publication Act, (1) The Chief Parliamentary Counsel shall, under the control of the Attorney-General, arrange for the printing and publication of (a) copies of every Act enacted by Parliament after the commencement

of this section; and (b) copies of all regulations made after the commencement of this section; and (c) reprints of Acts of Parliament and reprints of regulations; and (d) reprints of Imperial Acts that have effect as part of the laws of New Zealand.
(2) Every such copy and every such reprint shall state that it is published under the authority of the New Zealand Government.

This would appear to cover just about anything and everything coming out of Parliament, and it is intended to span the several individual publication requirements for specific kinds of documents and reports existing as early as 1908.[155] Similarly, Tanzania requires that every parliamentary bill be given a 21-day public notice period before its first reading so that there is time for community comment.[156]

In addition, New Zealand also expressly requires public notice concerning elections. These requirements have taken shape in the form of the Electoral Act of 1993, the Local Electoral Act of 2001, and the Electoral Amendment Act of 2002. The details include instructions about what the public notice must contain—"a statement about how persons interested in the proposals may inspect the full proposal"[157] and details about the nominations.[158]

In its constitution, Samoa requires more narrowly that candidates who have been elected to Parliament be declared as such in the *Samoa Gazette*.[159] But beyond that, the practice of public notice is relegated to individual agency practices. Mexico, too, is more careful with its constitutional references to public notice. It is generally referenced in requirements for local administration as "[t]he general bases of public municipal administration and administrative organs to settle the controversies which may arise between the administration and private parties, subject to the principles of equality, public notice, hearing, and legality."[160]

Kenya, too, requires written notice regarding elected position vacancies and election results. For example, in chapter 8 of Kenya's 2010 constitution, which covers the legislature, section 101 says:

(2) Whenever a vacancy occurs in the office of a member of the National Assembly under Article 97 (1) (*c*), or of the Senate under Article 98 (1) (*b*), (*c*) or (*d*), the respective Speaker shall, within twenty-one days of the occurrence of the vacancy, give notice in writing of the vacancy to—
(*a*) the Independent Electoral and Boundaries Commission; and
(*b*) the political party on whose party list the member was elected or nominated.
(3) A vacancy referred to in clause (2) shall, subject to clause (5), be filled in the manner prescribed by an Act of Parliament within twenty-one days of the notification by the respective Speaker.

> (4) Whenever a vacancy occurs in the office of a member of the National Assembly elected under Article 97 (1) (*a*) or (*b*), or of the Senate elected under Article 98 (1) (*a*)—
> (*a*) the respective Speaker shall, within twenty-one days after the occurrence of the vacancy, give notice in writing of the vacancy to the Independent Electoral and Boundaries Commission; and
> (*b*) a by-election shall be held within ninety days of the occurrence of the vacancy..."

The next section goes on to say:

> (2) Whenever a new House is elected, the President, by notice in the *Gazette*, shall appoint the place and date for the first sitting of the new House, which shall be not more than thirty days after the election.

And there are about a dozen more references to compulsory notice of government activities for the passage of laws and the internal actions of government officials.[161]

Sierra Leone, however, is specific about public notice regarding the purchase of goods for public use. Section 26 of its 2004 Procurement Act says:

> The procuring entity shall promptly publish in the Gazette and any newspaper of wide national circulation notice of each contract award in which the price of the contract exceeds the threshold set in the First Schedule, indicating the contract price and the name and address of the successful bidder.[162]

India has a complex body of laws, many of which require public notice, but among those of possible interest to the larger international community is the Biological Diversity Act of 2002.[163] The law provides for conservation of biological diversity, sustainable use of its components, and fair and equitable sharing of the benefits arising from the use of biological resources and knowledge about those matters. While public notice is not defined in this specific document, Chapter V, "Approval by the National Biodiversity Authority," unambiguously directs that "The National Biodiversity Authority shall give public notice of every approval granted by it" and that for the transfer of biological resource or knowledge, the Authority also "shall give public notice of every approval granted by it."

Similarly important to the wider international community might be Japan's Bankruptcy Act of 2004.[164] Public notice is required at every stage of the proceedings for court action in this law of more than 100 pages. What constitutes public notice within the authority of the act's Article 10 is as follows:

> (1) A public notice under the provisions of this Act shall be effected by publication in an official gazette.
> (2) A public notice shall become effective on the day following the day on which it is publicized.
> (3) Where a service is required to be made pursuant to the provisions of this Act, it may be substituted by a public notice; provided, however, that this shall not apply where both public notice and service are required to be made pursuant to the provisions of this Act.
> (4) When a public notice of a judicial decision is made pursuant to the provisions of this Act, it shall be deemed that all interested parties are notified of the judicial decision.

The act goes on to include requirements of public notice when there is a comprehensive prohibition order,[165] and, with the commencement of bankruptcy proceedings,[166] the following people must be informed of the situation:

> (3) (i) A bankruptcy trustee, the bankrupt, and known bankruptcy creditors, (ii) Known possessors of property, etc., (iii) A provisional administrator in cases where a provisional administration order prescribed in Article 91(2) is issued (iv) The labor union, etc. (meaning the labor union consisting of the majority of the bankrupt's employees and other workers, if there is any such labor union, or the person representative of the majority of the bankrupt's employees and other workers, if there is no labor union consisting of the majority of bankrupt's employees and other workers.

Public notice must also be given when there is a creditor's meeting,[167] a mediation order,[168] a liquidation order,[169] or a close-of-bankruptcy proceeding.[170]

There are also a number of bilateral treaties that mention public notice as portions of the agreements. The inclusion of the term is less a legal reference and more a generalization of community awareness. For example, the phrase is found in the following statement: "The calculation of such compensation shall not reflect any reduction in such fair market value due to either prior public notice of announcement of the expropriation action, or the occurrence of the events that constitute or result in the expropriation action."[171]

The use of public notice in this instance is a generic phrase referring to the more casual experience of community notary. The legal agreements that use public notice in this way include treaties between the United States and Senegal in 1983, between the United States and Congo in 1984, and between the United States and Bangladesh in 1986 ("Concerning the Reciprocal Encouragement and Protection of Investment"). Similarly, a treaty between the United States and South Korea includes the more general use of public notice in the import and export of certain kinds of products.[172]

Judiciary

Though the intention of including public notice as part of the legislative process varies from nation to nation, the result in almost every instance is to provide a sort of public awareness of the development and establishment of social order. Varying degrees of success can probably be found within each government as well as across nations, and the debate about who or what lies at fault for the public being unaware of government activities usually finds it way into the court system.

Courts have been adjudicating public notice requirements for centuries, and an early English case was open and shut, suggesting the sort of expectations the judges had about access to government documents. In the 1750 case *Herbert v. Ashburner*, the judgment says simply, "Every body has a right to inspect the books of the session." The details as reported in the court records include the following:

> Show cause why the defendant should not have liberty to inspect the books of the session of the Corporation of Kendale; it was objected, that the party is not entitled to see the books unless he can show to the Court by affidavit that they contain matters relating to the thing in question, which is, whether the park-lands be within the town or Corporation of Kendale?

The unanimous court response was loud and clear. "These are public books which every body has a right to see; and the rule was made absolute without hearing the other side."[173] Several generations later, the court again ruled that parishioners had the right to inspect the account books for the expenditures made by guardians of the poor. Chief Justice Lord Tenterden said, "We have no doubt that the party is entitled to inspect the books at a reasonable time.... The rule, therefore, must be absolute."[174] These courts clearly believed that public notice and access to public documents were necessities and not open to debate.

More recently, U.S. courts have reviewed the finer points of public notice in two major areas. One area of contention concerns where publication needs to occur. Another modern issue centers on what constitutes publication. Since the turn of the twenty-first century, at least a dozen state courts have reviewed the parameters for what qualifies as public notice, and some of these cases went to the state supreme courts. Here are just a few of the specific points in the cases.

- Were newspaper advertisements adequate notice?
- Were multiple forms of notice necessary?
- Did free newspapers meet the standard for legal notice posting?
- Was newspaper notice sufficient, or was actual notice required?
- Was the timing and frequency of the public notices sufficient?

As digital formats evolved into a preferred method of communication among government offices, the question about where publication occurred found its way into the courts. Almost without fail, the courts retained the centuries-old preference for paper-based publishing, but legislatures were soon offering bills that would change the law at the statutory level. In a survey of legislatures during the middle of the first decade of the twenty-first century, at least 34 states legislatures specifically included mention of traditionally published legal notice or public notice advertisement in at least 167 enacted bills that subsequently were signed into law during the period. In those states that sought and made changes in the law, there were at least 11 modifications that moved away from newspaper posting of notices. For example:

- Arizona allowed web posting of property sales (CH. 193 SB 1195);
- Georgia required that public notices for infrastructure development be published in regular pages rather than the classified pages for legal notice (Act 372 SB 200);
- Hawaii dropped the requirement that county tax revisions be published in the newspaper (Act 38 HB 2476) and decided that abandoned vehicle auctions for property valued at less than $1,000 need not be advertised in newspapers (Act 62 HB 2508);
- Illinois allowed web posting of legal notice for voter registration and election information where the municipal population was under 500,000 (Laws 645 HB 1968);
- Kansas ended the requirement that game population statistics and maps be published in newspaper ads (HB 2437);
- Kentucky now allows mail to carry a legal notice if it is more cost efficient than newspaper publication (CH. 47 SB 76);

- Nebraska decided that bond reports no longer need to be given public notice (Laws 206 City Treasurer);
- New Jersey allows certain school contracts for services to waive legal notice publication (Ch. 42 AN 17);
- Utah allows municipalities with budgets under $1M to forego legal notice publication of meetings, but newspaper ads are still required for most funding issues (Ch. 249 HB 222; Ch. 306 HB 264);
- Washington State allows web posting for project review committee meetings (HB 1506).

By the end of the decade, at least two dozen more bills were offered, and at least half of them were signed into law at the state level. They suggested the following changes to public notice laws:

- Idaho allowed electronic publishing to have the same legal effect as traditional publishing (60–106A);
- Nebraska allowed posting of notices on wall bulletin boards in addition to newspapers and also included special-interest newspapers as qualified publishers (33–141–142, (2010);
- New Jersey determined public notice was no longer required for certain kinds of purchases, including the contract for publishing public notices (40A:11–5(1)(j) (2011).
- On the other hand, New Mexico (14–11–10.2 (2010) and Wisconsin (Attorney General opinion) determined that web postings did not adequately substitute for legal notices where newspaper publication is required.

Newspapers and Public Notice

For at least two centuries, newspapers were the medium of legal choice for posting public notices. The reasons were as much about tradition as they were about principles. Newspapers functioned in many communities as a regularized bulletin board for local happenings.[175]

Though newspaper size, shape, distribution, rate, and management might be different from town to town or between countries, the ease of purchasing individual copies, sharing them with family or friends, carrying those copies as a traveling companion, and the ubiquity of the public newspapers' presence made them a natural candidate for popular reading and conversation. During much of the nineteenth and twentieth centuries, when many U.S. communities had multiple newspapers, there were countless political references to the power of the press in energizing citizen social engagement, and during the colonial period newspapers were unparalleled information sources.[176] Newspapers were relatively inexpensive and broadly distributed.

In countries where the government licensed the media, it was relatively easy for the courts to verify that the publishers were doing the job correctly. In those countries with unlicensed media, where they were reasonably separate from government, the courts could be sure of equal treatment no matter the political party in power. As Roger Sherman, an avid pamphleteer, put it in 1788, "The liberty of the press can be in no danger [in the United States] because that is not put under the direction of the new government."[177]

As a paid advertisement, the content was checked merely for format and obvious character errors, but the particulars of the message remained intact, as sworn by the newspaper organization. This made it routinely possible for individual pages from specific issues of the newspaper, called "tear sheets," to serve as validation of the public notice publication requirements. They provided a fixity that could later be summoned as a court document, and the routines of production made it possible and easy to track the progress and publication of the notice.[178]

This system worked rather well from the mid-1750s to the end of the twentieth century. Then the World Wide Web made it possible for notices to be posted for global distribution at what seemed like no cost and with no oversight. There were no deadlines for the publishers to meet, no finickiness about schedules, proofs, or corrections. This new platform for posting public notices seemed like the answer to many bureaucrats' prayers, except the courts were not sure this web posting met the requirements of public notice.

Executive branch officers often saw public notice as a nuisance to be borne, while courts saw it as a stopgap to actual notice. Political activists saw public notice as a much-needed window into government activity. During the initial period of the twenty-first century, each jurisdiction has spent time trying—with occasional success—to navigate the competing desires and intentions of public notice.

The intentions of public notice as a legal concept are narrower than the social intentions of courtesy public notices. Though this later version of public notice is very much a part of open societies, it is not the subject of this chapter. What we are concerned with immediately is handling the particulars of legal advertising, or meeting the needs of government-issued notices.

In summary, the law uses public notice published in newspapers when actual notice is not likely or possible. Courtesy public notices are not required by law, but instead draw attention to information that society wants to make broadly known. At the turn of the century, the relevant issues to be resolved if web posting were to replace newspaper publishing for legal-issue public notices included the following:

- Standardization of publication practices across platforms and jurisdictions;
- Elimination of geographic prescriptions for those served by the public notice publication;
- Standardization of format requirements for posting;
- Effective auditing of the reach and viewership for web posting of notices.

How, then, does the twenty-first-century bureaucrat or political activist sort through the variations to arrive at what might be expected of a government serving its constituents? In an attempt to discover what is available, the next several chapters will look at current norms and experiments. They are followed by a discussion of what might be adopted as principles for adequate public notice procedures in a world that expects quick access to information and stable platforms for presentation and review.

· 4 ·

MODERN EXAMPLES OF WEB POSTING

The previous chapters have provided an outline of the traditions—both social and legal—for public notice. This chapter will refine and build on our understanding of both the uses and values of public notice in an increasingly digital world by looking at examples as we find them on the World Wide Web.[179] Though the move to public notices on the web has not been codified by many governments, this platform is increasingly common around the world for both social and legal advertisements. It is sometimes used for no reason, often "just because" it is easy to do and quickly provides cover for the complaint that government operates in a vacuum.

For example, the website for New York's LaGuardia Airport carried a box headlined "Public Notice" with a letter attached that invited the air carriers of LaGuardia, John F. Kennedy International Airport, and Newark Liberty International Airport to attend allocation hearings for the use of "Apron Hardstand" funds to be collected through passenger facility charges.[180] An industrious reader of webpages might be able to make sense of why this matters and to whom, but by and large the casual viewer of the webpage probably left the link quickly to get back to any business at hand. In short, the use of this website for traditional public notification was probably minimal, and yet there it was.

Review of Public Notice Purpose

If the purpose of public notice is to make the business of government easily accessible at reasonable cost, then the web is a convenient solution to the distribution of whatever information is required for posting. Governments were quick to see the value of moving to web distribution for public notice, but, for obvious reasons, there was some resistance. The very elements that made newspaper distribution part of a good solution for so many years were not present in the web platform.

For nearly 300 years, newspapers were easily portable, easily read, easily saved, and quite inexpensive. On the other hand, the web—at the turn of the twenty-first century—was not yet easily and universally available. The equipment and subscriptions needed to access it in many places were still pretty expensive for public users, and the content, which was neither static not fixed, was easy to modify or change. Finally, storage server space for saving documents was still subject to shutdowns, burnouts, and data loss.

Governments tried a variety of web solutions during the late 1990s and early 2000s to make it work, often claiming that it would *eventually* be less expensive and easier to access, even if that weren't true just yet. Some governments tried direct posting to sponsored websites or government-supported hosts. But government activists countered that this allowed government to be unaccountable for late changes to the announcements—posting and changing the wording whenever it suited some bureaucrat. There was also concern that costs would run wild with little supervision as software and hardware changes were part of the web world, constantly undergoing development. When the webhost was an independent contractor, the concerns were about who owned the announcements and whether they would be available to the public as needed. Who would be accountable if everything just disappeared behind a paywall?

Public notices during the nineteenth and twentieth centuries had taken on a life as legal documents and were often part of court records. Most jurisdictions required that public notices be published in newspapers because the paper-based publications had most, if not all, of the following attributes:

- Printed in a fixed format
- Published on a regular basis for some long period of time
- Circulated to a known geographic area
- Offered for subscription at a low price

- Contained general news so that many would be interested, and could understand the publication
- Archived for easy access and for the life of the publication

Web presentations of an announcement, however, changed with each user interface and hardware setting. So, courts could not be sure that on any given day at any given desktop station, the announcement was clearly seen, or even seen the same way from desktop to desktop, for public viewing. These sorts of concerns slowed the quick adoption of public notice to the web environment, but within a decade many state governments and newspaper consortiums worked out the kinks enough so that the notices appeared in both print and web editions of newspapers, but were also searchable on the web for those who wanted only to see the announcements.

As a bonus, governments often claimed that public notice in newspapers was just a public subsidy to a private corporation that had not always been friendly to particular political parties. Posting on the web saved the taxpayer the public notice fees and stuck it to the newspapers, somewhat, at the same time. The question for most governments and civil activists seemed to be whether public notices on the web were effective in getting information to the public.

In a recent study asking just this question, researchers found that there was some correlation between the public's desire for government information and the preference for it to be provided online.[181] The study built on the work of a number of social scientists concerned with the kinds of information[182] and the credibility of the sources of government information as it is presented in a number of platforms.[183] This particular study, using 1,032 respondents from an online survey, was conducted in May 2012.[184] The results indicated the following.

> Support for publication of records...when seeking the most official source for education spending...[and] when asked of most trustworthy source for city council events...respondents [preferred] online forms of media over offline versions alongside [general] approval of public notice. When asked of media location preference for most trustworthy source of information on city council meetings, respondents [again preferred] online sources over offline in relation to approval of public notification. An analysis of variance found online sources to be the most preferred with the city council Website as the most trustworthy ($M = 1.46$, $SD = .77$). In a question seeking the most official source for information on local education spending, an analysis of variance exhibited significant preference for online sources—state government Website ($M = 1.38$, $SD = .80$), federal budget Website ($M = 1.33$, $SD = .83$)—over an offline source, the print version of hometown newspaper ($M = 1.13$, $SD = .86$); $F(3) = 7.49$, $p < .001$.

> In a post hoc multiple comparison, pairwise analysis found strong significant relationships between preference for the online version of hometown newspaper, the state government Website ($MD = -.45, p < .000$) and the federal budget Website ($MD = -.41, p < .000$). Pairwise relationships with the print version of hometown newspaper returned a significant relationship with the state government Website ($MD = -.25, p = .002$). Taken together, the questions show a clear preference for online sources in both most official and most trustworthy across a range of public, private, local, state, and federal entities.

This suggests that web users are more confident in government information published on the web than was once believed by researchers. It also appears that a government presence on the web is expected by most who use online resources. Public notice, if it is truly an aid to informing citizens about government activities in its various stages of completion, ought to be the first and best place to begin this process of migrating time-sensitive information from paper-based bulletin boards to wide distribution electronic forms.

Political Activists and Public Notice

Governments are not the only entities to find online public notice to be an engaging social, rather than legal, tool. Among the most striking web uses of public notice can be found in places where political activists have organized around an issue or political perspective. An example of that is the Website Public Notice at thepublicnotice.org, where the mission statement is all about supporting an informed population and is provided by an independent organization. The mission statement on the homepages reads as follows:

> Our goal is to provide Americans with clear, unbiased, and useful information about key economic and fiscal issues. Because America's future should rest in the capable hands of a knowledgeable people. Public Notice is an independent non-profit dedicated to providing facts and insight on the economy and how government policy affects Americans' financial well-being. Through education and awareness projects, Public Notice engages Americans on today's policies, to avoid tomorrow's problems. Americans, empowered with the facts, can lead Washington to be better stewards of the nation's economic and fiscal future.[185]

The site's links to projects and news reports focused on economic issues, and the page for terms of use of the site was by far the longest page attached to the website. Contact information was found as the last piece of information on that page, consisting of a post office box number, fax, phone, and email address. The only name attached to the website was the executive director,[186] who also was to receive copyright complaints. The executive director's descriptive resume was attached to a .com email address.[187]

Clearly, this is an example of the social use of public notice rather than the legal use. Under the "frequently asked questions" link was the following:

> *What is Public Notice?*
>
> Public Notice is an independent, non-partisan, non-profit organization dedicated to providing facts and insight on the economy and how government policy affects Americans' financial well-being.
>
> *Are we Republicans? Democrats?*
>
> No, we are a non-partisan independent organization that holds both sides accountable. Government has been overspending for years, under the auspices of Republicans and Democrats. If you read through our blog and watch our videos, you will find that we criticize both parties for engaging in irresponsible spending. The Bankrupting America project seeks to inform and engage citizens with regard to the threat posed by unsustainable and misguided government spending. We will champion the ideas of anyone who seeks to help in our efforts, regardless of the letter beside their name.[188]

While the fundamental intention of the website is to provide information so that a political constituency is fully informed, this social use of the term "public notice" is overbroad for the content—economics. Knowledge of economics theory and practice is always an interesting framework for judging the activities of government, but not the only way in which to talk about success or failure of a particular nation-state. Many successful social systems use economic levers in very different ways with very different intentions and very different priorities than this particular site espouses. Public notice here is intended to operate more in the realm of headlines than heads up.

A contrasting website was launched in January 2013 that claims the universe of public notice, both legal and social. The URL (universal resource locator) for this site sits on a .com called "noticeandcomment," or Notice & Comment. The "how to use this site" page reports that there are more than 37,000 special district governments and 52,000 general-purpose government entities that must publish public notices. What the site offers is a one-stop resource for finding the more than 17 million notices published each year.[189] It also suggests that public notice advocates will be best served by a site like this one.

> NoticeandComment.com enhances the "watchdog" role of citizens and organizations by empowering them to influence outcomes, generate greater support for their views, and participate more effectively in one of the nation's oldest democratic traditions—civic participation. No more problems finding the right local newspaper containing the public notice ad on an obscure back-page. Instead, the public can conveniently use this site to shape the proposed actions that affect them and their wallets…and they can do it from anywhere….
>
> Following the lead of regulations.gov, we post only official notices, ensure local governments maintain control over all notice postings, and allow them to participate on our site for free. As a non-partisan communications utility, we take no sides and thus there's no political risk for local governments to join. In return, the nation can benefit from our unique database of public sentiment, trends and tipping points, which is the heart of good civic analysis and decision-making.
>
> Civic modernization, new money for new projects and better communications: all within one revolutionary idea. NoticeandComment.com, "*where politics end and your Governance begins*."[190]

The site segregates local from federal notices and includes press releases.[191] Though site data were unavailable at mid-year, the site looked to be considerably below national levels of published public notices, showing tens of thousands rather than the hundreds of thousands it suggested were probable in a single year. Though the site lists several partners, it seems likely that it will be some time before all governments at every level jump on this opportunity for broad distribution.

How, then, might customs and use of public notice be reasonably reviewed if social and legal contexts are co-mingled? What mechanisms could be employed to identify those instances of the legal system *requiring* public notice rather than the social system *expecting* public notice? Does the separation really matter if the point of public notice is to attract attention and promote engagement in the social system, either legal or functional?

Governments and Online Public Notice

The following sections will be differentiated by geographic region and country rather than by strict legal requirements or the softer social norms. Grouping in this way will help us organize what we find, realizing that sometimes neighbors do share social traits and common histories. Though countries within regions shift, regions grouped under broad headings generally remain about the same.[192] Those regions include Africa, Asia, Europe, the Americas, the Middle East, and Oceania (including Australia).

Near the end of the chapter some general observations will be made about what sorts of content seem to receive consistent public notice attention across countries to determine if there might be some commonalities about what people everywhere expect from their government and their social organizations. In this way the author hopes to provide a stepping-off point for development of a template that might be used as an international tool for public notice, no matter the specifics of government framing or social strictures. If this template could solve the problem of international notice, there might at last be some sense of safety for knowing what most needs to be known as a citizen of the world.

Africa

A continent of more than 1 billion people comprising nearly 60 sovereign states, Africa has as wide a variety of government forms as any continent in the world. Northern Africa is claimed by some to be the cradle of civilization among those groups living along the Nile River. Among socializing governments, it is undeniable that the obelisks of the region were a reminder to all who saw them that the government of the local residents was doing the work expected of higher beings.[193]

Today the countries of Africa include some characterized as tribal fiefdoms and some as emerging democracies. Many of the countries self-identify as republics, or as representative democracies in which the people's elected deputies (representatives), not the people themselves, vote on legislation. This is a government structure that would be very interested in a purposive, legal use of public notice. Yet what is found is a smattering of public notices on a variety of topics. The following is a sample.

Algeria, with a population of about 37 million and a projected Internet user[194] population of 5 million,[195] posted a broad English-language public notice in 2008 inviting parties who wanted to set up a 3G mobile communication network in cooperation with the Algerian Regulation Authority of Post and Telecommunication (ARPT) to review the application procedures posted at a URL.[196] There seemed to be, however, a more limited follow-up on the ARPT homepage in either French or Algerian.[197] More recently the Algerian government posted a notice to its citizens living abroad stating that

> Algerian citizens registered with the Embassy of Algeria are hereby informed that Law 12–12 dated Dec. 26, 2012 (Finance Law for 2013) provides in Article 31 that provisions of Article 202 of Law 79–07 of July 21, 1979, as amended and completed, establishing the Customs Code, have been amended to read as follows:
>
> Article 202: Algerian citizens registered with diplomatic and consular posts overseas and returning for good to their homeland are entitled to export the following free of charge, provided they can demonstrate continuous residence of at least three years in their country of residence, at the date of application for a Statement of Residency Change, known as C.C.R.: (…)
>
> 2. Text should end as follows: (…) vehicles must be new at date of shipping. A. Items listed above shall clear customs and shall be exempted from foreign trade control and any related levies and taxes, when value of said items, including the vehicle, does not exceed two million Algerian Dinars (2,000,000.00 DA) for trainees and students and three million Algerian Dinars (3,000,000.00) for all other returning citizens.[198]

These are very limited uses of public notice—one is an invitation to participate and the other is a reminder of how a specific law has changed. Neither suggests a regularization of notification.

Nigeria, with a population of more than 170 million and an Internet user base estimated at 48 million, posts both government public notices and social notices. Similar to the broadly posted notice by Algeria mentioned above, the Central Bank of Nigeria posted the following:

> This is for the information of everyone. CENTRAL BANK OF NIGERIA Public Notice.
>
> The attention of the Central Bank of Nigeria (CBN) has been drawn to the activities of some persons (individuals and members of the public) under the guise of subscription to venture partnership arrangements with a promise to subscribers of sharing profits with owners of the company at mouth watering interest rates of up to for example =N=40,000.00 (or 8.8%) for =450,000.00 per month or other agreed periods.
>
> The CBN is concerned about this worrisome development reminiscent of the past "Umanah-Umanah" scheme which masqueraded as wonder bank. Consequently, the CBN wishes to reiterate that only licensed banks, mortgage finance institutions and micro finance banks are authorized to take deposits from the public while discount and finance houses are allowed to borrow from the public and pay interest through their money market products.
>
> In view of the above, members of the public are advised to be wary of this kind of financial arrangement as anyone who subscribes to such scheme does so, at his/her own risk.

Furthermore, any bank which provides a vehicle for such fund mobilization should ensure that it does not breach the provisions of the know your customer (KYC) guidelines issued by CBN.

Source: Financial Standard, Monday, July 9, 2007, page 45.[199]

More formally, the Nigerian Copyright Commission posted a remembrance of World Intellectual Property Day in 2013,[200] and the Nigerian Electricity Regulation Commission posted a list of the successful applicants for metering implementation—both announcements noted as public notices—as well as the Tenure for Licenses Notification, Notice of the Review of 2012 Retail and Distribution Tariff Order, Issue Guidelines for Derogation from Electricity Codes and Standards, Notice of Rulemaking of Health and Safety Code, Notice of the Development of Regulations and Guidelines to Govern Nigeria National Content Development in the Nigerian Electrical Supply Industry 2013, Regulatory Meetings of the Commission in 2013, and many more such notices.[201]

Morocco, with a population of 32 million and a projected Internet user population of 16 million, also uses public notices for a range of government activity, though its government is identified as a constitutional monarchy rather than a representative democracy. The depth of posting includes things such as the entire 290-page, 2010 Maroc Telecom registration document.[202] But the breadth of postings is rather narrow, given that nearly 50% of the country's population is said to be Internet users.[203] For example, the "Address to the Nation by His Majesty King Mohammed VI on the occasion of the 55th Anniversary of the Revolution of the King and the People" was posted in several languages.[204] The national port authority provides a searchable website.[205] A manual for the procedures of family justice was available,[206] and there was a web portal for family services.[207] As one might expect from a monarchy, there is less emphasis on societal input and more emphasis on the areas of service provided by government.

Among the more brightly lit examples of social media's effects on governance in the early twenty-first century is Egypt. During the Arab Spring revolutions throughout northern Africa and the Middle East, Egypt's population used social media to identify gathering places and call together protesters.[208, 209] With a population of 83 million and an estimated 30 million Internet users, Egypt is among the most web-savvy countries. Until the changes in government leadership in 2011, however, the day-to-day use of the web for government activity was unremarkable. In 2003 Egypt launched the "Information Portal" where "Information Access Is a Right for Each Citizen,"[210] but the site has since been updated to include feedback from users in almost every area of viewership.

On another section of the government portal, the Information and Decision Support Center, finance reports, policy briefs, poll results, and even an opportunity to provide a spot vote all are available.[211]

Here is an example of the spot vote that was viewable on June 5, 2013:

What is the extent of your response for calls for rationalization of electricity consumption?

◯ **I always respond**

◯ **Sometimes I try to respond**

◯ **I refuse to respond**

Vote | Previous Votes

The Middle East

This region of the world is the least populated but generally holds a very high concentration of Internet users. There are roughly 200 million residents within about a dozen nations, and in 2012 it was estimated that almost 90 million of them were Internet users. Iran alone was believed to have 42 million of its population of 78 million regularly online. Iraq was estimated to have the lowest percentage of users.[212] Though only a few of the countries in the region are identified as democracies or republics of any sort, the range of Internet use and the percentage of users differ radically within this small group of nations. As mentioned, Iraq reports that only 7% of its population is online, while Israel appears to have nearly 70% of its 7.5 million residents online.

In Iraq there were plenty of public notices posted online but not by the formal government.[213] In a notice dated June 5, 2003, a PDF version of an announcement by the Office of Coalition Provisional Authority prohibited any kind of incitement. Similarly, an undated public notice by the provisional authority announced the establishment of the Iraq Central Bank Development Fund.[214] More recently, however, Iraq has been posting reports and business announcements[215] that include statements like the following:

> The ISX [Iraq Securities Exchange] shall provide at least 30 days public notice of an auction for new memberships, subject to the minimum price determined as set forth above, and shall conduct such auction subject to terms and conditions to be approved by the Commission.[216]

This small sampling is in contrast to Israel's web public notice presence, which is wide and deep. Easily located are the usual reports and law changes, but also present are notices about health practitioners,[217] airport authority practice drills,[218] or changes in welfare center hours of operation, with a "tell a friend" application on pages such as this one:

> To allow the Welfare Department to prepare for 2013, the welfare center at Olim Center (8 Tel Hai St.) will be closed to the public on Sunday–Thursday, December 23–27, 2012. At the Young Women's Service (32 Shmuel Hanatziv St.) on Monday–Thursday, December 24–27, 2012, and at the Mizrach Welfare Center (22 Weizmann St.) on Tuesday–Thursday, December 24–27, 2012.[219]

Since Israel is described as a parliamentary democracy, its broad use of websites to provide government news is not a surprise. Less obvious, however, is the fact that some of the region's monarchies and emirates are also home to a high percentage of Internet users and a wide government web presence. For example, Kuwait's population of about 2.6 million also has nearly 2 million Internet users. Qatar's population of almost 2 million has about 1.6 million Internet users. Similarly, Bahrain, with 1.2 million residents, has about 1 million Internet users.[220] Though these governments do not routinely use web postings to engage civil discourse, the infrastructure is there, and the population is well versed in web communication.

Europe

This region, for our purposes, reaches from Albania and Turkey through Sweden, the United Kingdom, and Portugal. Though home to only about 10% of the world's population, it hosts about 20% of the world's Internet users. On average, about 60% of European residents are Internet users, with the northern countries comprising the highest percentages of users. An exception to that generalization is Monaco, which reports that 100% of its population uses the Internet.

The range of government structures across the nearly 50 countries is quite variable. And as in the Middle East, type of government does not categorically indicate likelihood of Internet use. Denmark, Sweden, and Norway, with constitutional monarchies, count more than 90% of their populations as Internet users. On the other hand, many emerging democracies—such as Bosnia-Herzegovina, Hungary, and Lithuania—count closer to 60% of their populations as Internet users. Turkey, with one of the higher populations of a republican parliamentary democracy—almost 80 million—has one of the lower percentages of Internet users, about 36 million.

Form of government is clearly not the sole predictor of web use, either by a government or its citizens. For example, Turkey, with a relatively low Internet user population, posts a wide range of public notices on the web. From the material safety data sheets at the Yeosu LG Plant[221] and the Ministry of Foreign Affairs business residency requirements,[222] to the Turkish Academy of Sciences establishment documents[223] and the public thank-you to student participants in a television commercial campaign against child abuse and street beggars,[224] the government of Turkey is making headway in posting both legal and social public notices on the web.

Monaco also has a high web presence, but the web pages primarily offer information about services rather than about governance. For example, there are pages to help those who are in need of relocation services[225] or are establishing a business[226]—even those who want to nominate someone for public honors.[227] There were public service announcements, including notices as to when stamps went on sale[228] and a list of public holidays.[229] By and large, the postings were all announcements or updates of what the government provided citizens rather than opportunities for citizens to shape the government's actions, which is not surprising in a constitutional monarchy, no matter how high the percentage of Internet users in the country.

Perhaps most typical of what one might expect is evident in the website materials posted by Germany and France. Though slightly different in the details of their government structure, both are republics, and both count about 80% of their populations as Internet users. Government public notices range from urban renewal[230] and public comment[231] to public talks about services available[232] and town schedules of activities[233] in France. And in Germany it is easy to find public notices of warnings about product malfunctions[234] and shareholder documents,[235] as well as historical documents with international provisions for aircraft property rights from the 1940s and 1950s.[236]

Though the governments have varying needs for public notice, the many uses and the relatively high proportion of Internet users suggest a strong expectation of posting information on the web for both public consumption and civic engagement.

Oceania

The overall population of this region is estimated to be about 36 million, roughly 0.5% of the world's population, but its share of Internet users is about 1% of the worldwide total. Australia, the principal continent among a range of islands in the region, is home to the largest population in the area by far. Its 22 million residents include 19 million Internet users, in contrast to Papua New Guinea's population of 6 million with merely 100,000 Internet users. New Zealand is home to 4 million people, nearly all of whom are Internet users. Though many of the governments in Oceania are part of the British Commonwealth or protectorates of the United States, many have small Internet-using populations.

Australia and New Zealand, as noted in many examples provided earlier in this book, have robust websites for both government and social public notices. In fact, the Australian government posted a note to this effect:

> The Australian Government is increasingly using the internet to provide a channel for public consultations on specific topics. These consultations link to agency Websites where the relevant agency has published a discussion or consultation paper, which can be responded to via the internet or by postal mail. These public consultations are targeted to anyone who is interested as well as experts, peak bodies and interest groups. Using the internet for public consultations enables government to engage more directly and widely with the public in the development of citizen-centered policy and programs.[237]

And that government has a regular publication called the *Gazette* for the various public notices. Here is the web post describing the *Gazette's* various iterations:

> The Government Notices Gazettes, including Special and Periodic Gazettes, are published by ComLaw.
>
> **Government Notices Gazette**
> The regular Government Notices Gazette is published each Wednesday and contains a range of notices including information about legislation, notices of Australian Government Departments, Courts notices, and other notices required under Commonwealth law.
>
> **Special Notices Gazette**
> The Special Notices Gazette normally contains a single notice, and may be published at any time. Special Notices Gazettes published during the week are republished at the end of the next regular Government Notices Gazette.
>
> **Periodic Notices Gazette**
> The Periodic Notices Gazette is published irregularly and may contain multiple notices relating to a specific subject area.[238]

The Australian government also supports some special interest gazettes for public service, business, securities and investments, tariff concessions, chemicals, pesticides, and veterinary medicines, and food standards. Each has its own web presence.

Similarly, New Zealand hosts a government *Gazette* with the following purpose and schedule. The website for the *Gazette* also provides a native-language presentation.

> The *New Zealand Gazette* is the official newspaper of the Government of New Zealand and is produced every Thursday (except over Christmas/New Year) by the New Zealand Gazette Office at the Department of Internal Affairs.
>
> Each edition of the *New Zealand Gazette* is divided into commercial and government notices, covering business proceedings, bankruptcies, land transfer notices, departmental and parliamentary notices.
>
> The *New Zealand Gazette* office also publishes a Customs Edition every Tuesday, Special Editions, Supplements, Professional and Trade Lists, and Bound Volumes.
>
> **Gazette Notices**
> This site offers a searchable database of all Gazette notices from September 1993. To access this database visit Gazette Notices.
>
> Alternatively, you can access pdf versions of all Gazette editions since 2000. Our aim is to upload the pdf files of Gazette editions every Friday. Please note that this may not always be possible.[239]

Apart from the government public notices, however, there are the usual sorts of announcements posted in the local newspapers, both in print format and on the web. There were dozens posted in the *New Zealand Herald* on a given day, ranging from advertisements for employment to death announcements. Here is a sampling:

> **NGA URI O HANA HOROMONA TAUHINU TRUST**
> A G.M 1. Election of Commitee 2. Lease of Tongariro 3A Saturday 15 June 2013, 9am to 11am, Papatuanuku Marae, Robertson…
> Published Thursday, June 13, 2013
>
> **NOTICE OF AGM**
> Wharawhara 3b2 Shareholders are hereby notified that the Wharawhara 3B2 Ahu Whenua Trust AGM will be held on Saturday 15th…
> Published Thursday, June 13, 2013

NOTICE OF APPLICATION FOR AUCTIONEER'S LICENCE I
Barrie Raymond Bogue of 41 Lilburn Street, Warkworth, Auckland, hereby give notice that I have applied to the District Court...
Published Thursday, June 13, 2013

NOTICE OF APPOINTMENT OF RECEIVERS AND MANAGERS OF SKDJ TRUST
(In Receivership) The Mortgagors: Kyung Hye Kim (also known as Seselia Kim), Dong Jin Kim (also known as Allan Kim) and...
Published Thursday, June 13, 2013

NOTICE OF INTENTION TO REMOVE COMPANY FROM REGISTER IN THE MATTER of The Companies Act 1993 and IN THE MATTER of BREAM TAIL FARM LIMITED (IN LIQUIDATION) NOTICE is hereby given in...
Published Thursday, June 13, 2013

R126
(b), 263(1) G10 NOTICE BY ADVERTISEMENT In the Family Court at Auckland FAM-2013–004–001176 To: Chao Hsiung Ku Manee Kaewta...
Published Thursday, June 13, 2013

R126
(B), 263(1) G10 NOTICE BY ADVERTISEMENT In the Family Court at Auckland FAM-2012–004–003537 To: Christine Gail Mcleod Glenn...
Published Thursday, June 13, 2013

THE AGM OF THE NZ BAKERS AND PASTRYCOOKS UNION INC
Will be held at Silver Oaks Lodge, Allenby Park 477 Great South Road Papatoetoe Auckland Thursday 27th June 2013 at 11.00am...
Published Thursday, June 13, 2013

WOULD JASPER HANNAY OF NEWERA ELECTRICAL
39B TOMO STREET, GLEN EDEN (Last known contact address) Please contact Safestore Containers re storage, within seven (7)...
Published Thursday, June 13, 2013

WOULD ROBERT HOGARTH OF 39B SOUTH LYNN RD
NEW LYNN (Last known contact address) please contact Safestore Containers re storage, within seven (7) days of publication...
Published Thursday, June 13, 2013

Of the smaller nations, or those with far fewer Internet-using populations, Papua New Guinea is a good example of the scattering use of public notice. Banks,[240] government land management offices,[241] telecommunications,[242] and ports[243] often use public notice as a means of announcing changes or closures, but such notices are not embraced systematically across government entities for notification or as a way to engage civil discourse. Private entities, too, use public notice as a way to circulate their news, but it is not expected to provide a binding legal environment.[244]

The Americas

Though the Americas comprise only 13% of the world's population, the region is home to 22% of the world's Internet users. North Americans make up more than half the number of web users, though they constitute only about one-third of the region's population. Of the more than 50 sovereign states in the region, the vast majority identify as republics of some sort—the most obvious exception being Cuba. Yet most of these countries do not support a government-sponsored public notice system.

In picturesque Belize, the Department of Environment seems to be among a handful of entities posting any kind of public notice reports, and those reports that appear are few in number.[245] The Board of Elections did post the revisions of laws that included the following about public notice:

> Public Notices Respecting Payments By Public
> 28. Notices shall be displayed warning the public not to pay monies to officers without obtaining an official receipt and pointing out that such receipt is the only discharge accepted.[246]

A surprising exception is notification from the World Trade Organization that Belize had established public notice standards for trade documents in 2010. These notices require distribution in at least two newspapers and a waiting period of months in order to allow time for public comment.[247]

A majority of the countries of South America are identified as republics or parliamentary democracies. As this would suggest, there are a variety of ways in which these governments inform their citizens about the work of government. Though most of these countries are not English-language nations, they have a surprising number of host sites for public notice in English.

Argentina, with almost two-thirds of its 42 million residents identified as Internet users, hosts a number of public notice portals, through both government and private channels. Banks advertise bond meetings,[248] companies notify communities about their good citizenship,[249] and the government posts regulations, in one example for garment labeling.[250] Brazil, with its estimated 88 million Internet users—nearly half of its population—also posts public notice in a variety of ways. The Ministry of External Affairs wanted the world to know about an essay competition[251] and to announce experimental initiatives for easing poverty.[252] Similarly, youth day initiatives were posted by the São Paulo Sacred Art Museum.[253] Peru, with a much smaller population of just under 30 million and about 10 million Internet users, posts U.S. trade remedy agreements in English,[254] and private companies post pre-shipment inspection requirements in English.[255]

Much of this book has already been devoted to similar examples in the United States, so little of that landscape will be noted here. Suffice it to say that Mexico uses legal notices and public notices in much the same way as the United States. For example, local announcements are just as easily found[256] as company[257] and national government notices.[258] Though Mexico is home to about 114 million residents, only about one-third are believed to be Internet users. Canada, on the other hand, with a population of about 34 million, identifies about 80% of its population as Internet users, and the United States classifies about 80% of its more than 300 million residents as Internet users. Both Canada and the United States use web posts at all levels of government and, increasingly, for all aspects of government information.

Asia

This region of the world is home to more than half the global population but less than one-third of its Internet users. The countries that make up Asia are as variable as in any area of the world, and include both very dense groupings of Internet users and areas with none at all. Myanmar, with more than 54 million residents, appears to have about only 1% who are Internet users, while South Korea's 48 million inhabitants are thought to include more than 40 million Internet users. Though China boasts the highest population of the region at more than 1 billion, it is estimated that only 40%, or about 538 million, are Internet users. Still, that 538 million for China exceeds many other regions combined. For example, the Middle East, Africa, and North America together total only about 530 million Internet users.

Public notice finds a number of uses among the region's English-language countries. India is by far the most comprehensive legal notice state, with many social public notice outlets. The web platform for the *Times of India* published articles regularly that were tagged as public notices. These included alerts to the public about job opportunities, as well as directives by government officers that beach shacks be removed.[259] Classified or line ads were commonly part of the daily paper, reaching nearly 40 million in multiple languages. Examples include notices of name change, death, marriage, property transfer, and a range of personal issue announcements. These are somewhat in keeping with the types of announcements found in many Western newspapers carrying public notice ads, but quite different from those found in other parts of Asia.

In China, public notices are largely handled by private practitioners such as attorneys' offices. An example is the recent web publication of a disagreement about how to handle ownership of some kinds of assets. The attorneys involved in the dispute took the documents and issues to the web—not for adjudication, but simply to distribute pertinent information to those who might need to know.[260] Other examples include those from private companies alerting the public to product concerns.[261] Both Taiwan and Singapore, each associated with mainland China in a very different way, are home to 23 million and 5 million residents respectively, and each has a high penetration of Internet use—about 75%. Given this, one might expect a higher incidence of web-form public notice. However, it is easier to find public notices from the early 1900s than from the twenty-first century. The Singapore National Library hosts a searchable site for public notices, but the newspapers are less forthcoming.[262] This is in sharp contrast to Taiwan's more easily available government-sponsored and private corporation postings.[263]

Asia, unlike many of the other regions described here, does not seem to have an enthusiastic relationship with either public notice or government-sponsored web posting. In this region, too, the size of the country's population does not necessarily pair with high Internet use. Given the two extremes of highly controlled government web use and a more free-ranging private web use, the place for public notice is quite variable, and the expectation of web placement for public notices similarly lacks a fixed pattern.

Conclusions

Though the regions described here vary in many ways, there are some similarities in the ways that public notices are treated on the web. For example, several governments, including Algeria, used the web for posting public notices about how particular laws needed to be observed by those who might reside beyond the country's borders. Most of the countries that hosted web posting also used public notice notation as a way of focusing attention on important information for residents and citizens alike. From Canada to Costa Rica, Morocco to Monaco, Switzerland to Swaziland, many countries posted public notices to highlight elements of government activity that make the work look positive and affirming.

Much less often did governments use the web to actively engage public comment. As noted, Israel and Egypt, some of the northern European countries, and some of those in the Americas, as well as Australia and New Zealand in the Oceania region, ranked highest in the frequency with which the web postings of public notice seemed to be aimed at eliciting public response.

As may be clear from the regional descriptions above, the form of government did not dictate the use of web public notices, though the frequency and range of such postings seemed higher among those nations where government requires a high degree of public engagement. Among the surprises, however, was the fact that Turkey has such a wide use of web public notices despite the fact that the population is so lightly engaged in Internet use, according to a survey made in 2012.

Perhaps the most important observation provided by the above roundup is that there are no obvious, clear-cut correlations between government types and web posting of public notices. Some emerging democracies and some long-established monarchies are equally engaged in public notices as a means of informing the public about what government is doing for them. Further, it is apparent that the more vigorous the representative democracy, the higher the likelihood that web postings of public notice will also be used to engage or solicit activist participation in directing government activities.

Though there may not be any consistency in the number or range of public notices a particular government posts, there is evidence to suggest that, in the early twenty-first century, many citizens in these kinds of representative government organizations expect web posting. In fact, not only do they expect it, but they also seem to be willing to forgive some of the strictures of long-held traditions in public notice laws in order to have the convenience of Internet access to the reports and detailed information that governments use to make decisions on behalf of constituents.

· 5 ·

COSTS FOR PUBLIC NOTICE

The principles and history of public notice have been presented in previous chapters, but what has not yet been discussed is the cost of producing and distributing these announcements. While the staff resources dedicated to the production of public notice are often slight, the cost of placing a notice in the appropriate publication seems to rankle some government activists. These expenses, in comparison to those triggered by freedom of information and open access requirements, where citizens make requests and entire offices are required to respond, are actually quite small. Nonetheless, this practice of reporting on social and political communities by means of public notice doesn't happen for free.

Many proponents of changing the public notice system have urged moving publication to the web because, it is claimed, costs will be lowered and there will be less work involved in producing and publishing the notices. There are also claims that web distribution by its very nature will be more inclusive because it is wider, and that the response from the public will, as a result, be more robust. Questions about the population served by web distribution, the costs of server and distribution list upkeep, and the general requirements of preserving the public records so that they are accessible and accurately reproduced across the years are usually left unmentioned in the pleas for a shift to digital distribution. The true benefits of web posting have not yet been put to the test, so this chapter will instead examine what the costs have been for the existing system of public notice.

Privately Owned Newspaper Model

Some countries' government notices have for centuries been published through privately owned newspapers as legal advertisements, and the government is issued a bill for this service. For example, in the United States there is a well-developed system of public notice publication at the state and federal levels. Newspapers in this system apply for "record" or "legal" status by meeting a list of requirements to win the designation. Usually there is at least one and often several such newspapers named within a governmental district so that public notice requirements can always be met.

The criteria for becoming a record newspaper or a legal newspaper, depending on the designation used by a particular state, usually include some or all of the following:

- Regular publication for more than a year;
- Frequent publication;
- In English (or local language);
- Guaranteed level of paid subscribers;
- Distribution in the government district;
- Meets and maintains requirements of federal second-class mailing materials;
- Standard newspaper size and typeface;
- Majority of content is news of general interest or legal news;
- Produced and published within or near the government district to be served;
- Archived for producing "tear sheets" or facsimile copies on demand.

These requirements were more extensively reviewed in Chapter 3, but, to recap, the list noted here was not randomly created. The purpose of many of these elements was to assure some stability in the process of public notice and to ensure exposure for the announcement in a place where it was most likely to be relevant. For example, regular publication and frequent publication in standard newspaper format where the content is primarily news facilitates a social habit of seeing and noting the announcements. Paid subscribers increase the likelihood of continued regular publication and a degree of public exposure for the notices. Distribution in the geographic area affected by the public announcements, again, aid in the probability that those who need to know about government activity will actually see the notice. Meeting federal second-class mailing standards and archiving tear sheets promote accountability.

Web posting could meet many of these criteria under some conditions, but the difficulties in rethinking the social values of the legal conditions for record newspaper status has kept most government activists at bay. There are legislative members who repeatedly offer bills for consideration that either eliminate public notice altogether or severely curtail publication. The rationale usually offered is that public notice is a costly government activity that serves no purpose. Often these efforts are accompanied by additional bills that provide for posting on government-sponsored websites or the homepages of the particular agencies that believe they benefit from the contract bidding process, for example, or that care to continue the practice of public notice at all.

Following debate or the advice of an attorney general, the legislative attacks on public notice are sometimes quietly shelved or outright defeated. In state court challenges to bills that have gained passage, judges often return to the conservative past and strike down these efforts to post only on agency webpages.[264] The court opinions often cite the long history of public notice norms within the jurisdiction and go on to reiterate the values of public notice as a means of providing, even though sometimes minimally, public observation of government at work.

There are a few instances in which states have successfully opted for narrow applications of web publication alone. Early in the twenty-first century these included, for example, Idaho, which allows electronic publishing under some conditions,[265] and Kentucky, which added the broadcasting of notices in order to supplement printing notices.[266] Nebraska voted to allow some notices to be posted on the physical walls of government office bulletin boards rather than be published in newspapers,[267] and Missouri decided it was appropriate to mail notices to individuals in locations where there were fewer than 750 registered voters.[268]

New Jersey decided to eliminate public notice requirements for certain sorts of purchases, including the contracts for publishing public notice.[269] And in 2009 the U.S. Department of Justice, spurred on by the possibility of millions of dollars in savings, announced that it would post judicial property seizure notices on the web only.[270]

About half the states in the United States have elected to post public notices on local government websites in addition to publishing the announcements in the usual paper-format newspapers. Several consortiums have organized to post these state-level public notices either in concert with the existing newspapers or alongside the established "record" publications. Some examples include PublicNoticeAds.com and myPublicNotices.com.

PublicNoticeAds.com's banner proclaims the message "Access information that is 'your right to know.'" It also notes that the site is hosted by the organization Newspapers of America. Just below the banner is a declaration smaller typeface that "The public notice database on this site is not a substitute for the official publication that is required by law. You will still find those notices in your local newspaper."[271] The site notes that not all states are represented in the database, and it provides links directly to each state. It also offers a free subscription to a service that will automatically deliver public notices to an email address.

MyPublicNotices.com reports on its homepage that it is hosted in collaboration with participating newspapers and provides a search window for dates, categories, keywords, and states. Again, not all states were represented at the time of recent viewing, but the site did include more than just legal advertisements and noted for the purposes of this site that public notices include community information and

> inform you about government actions, environmental conditions and economic changes. Public notices alert you when the interests of your family, your neighborhood or your business are affected by what others do. Public notices invite you to participate in the democratic process and in business opportunities.[272]

Government-Owned Newspaper Model

There are a number of countries that publish government-owned newspapers for distribution of, among other things, public notices, and in these cases it is a bit more difficult to break out the exact cost of the announcements. For example, New Zealand's government directly supports the *New Zealand Gazette* published every Thursday. It is the official newspaper of the government and is available both in print and on the web. On the website for disclosures, the *Gazette* reminds those who are concerned about privacy that "once information is published in the New Zealand Gazette it becomes a 'notice to the world' and cannot be amended or withdrawn."[273]

Not only does the *Gazette* website provide public notices as the announcements are made for both government and commercial interests, but it also links to aggregate data for easy access on such topics as government ministers' expenses, local authority development contributions, the expenses of the department of internal affairs' chief executive, gaming machine statistics, and the most popular male and female first names.[274]

While not all of these databases are of critical importance for government operations, the site suggests that government takes very seriously its responsibility to provide as much information as possible about New Zealand's social indicators as might be of interest to any of the country's residents. So serious, in fact, are the editors of the *Gazette* about providing the public with information that there is also a page reporting statistics on government data queries and the number of views and unique viewers of the public notice pages and databases.[275]

Though this kind of relationship between government and its published public notices seems wholesome, there were reasons that the organizers of the United States emphatically chose to keep government and the public notice independent of one another. Accountability and suspicion of bureaucrats were repeatedly voiced as concerns during the Constitutional Convention and in the early days of Congress. A glance back through history finds many examples to warrant such concern.[276]

Privately Owned Web Publication Model

A search of the web for public notice sites that are not government sponsored and are not limited to particular domestic nations or narrow consumer topics elicited only a handful of results.[277] These included, in the early twenty-first century, http://i-uv.com/post-your-courtesy-notices-for-the-world-community-to-acknowledge/, a site that provided free space for "all people who wish to give 'public notice' To Who It May Concern."[278]

The website http://www.globaltenders.com/index.htm, from India, was more focused, providing posting services from clients in dozens of countries around the world who were interested in contract work.[279] The subscribers were offered a variety of plans for viewing the bidding announcements that ranged from year-round unlimited access to limited viewing for 30 days. The sources of the notices were "newspapers, journals, magazines, [and] genuine government websites across the globe."[280] contrast, London's *Financial Times* hosts a legal notice blog that serves clients with questions about how and when to post worldwide public notices.[281]

Government-Owned Web Publication Model

The government-owned websites for public notice publication were most frequently found among the monarchies with parliaments or houses of representatives. This was most common among the European and Middle Eastern nations, as well as many of the developing democracies of Africa. For example, Monaco supports an extensive and easily navigated website for public notices about both business and individuals[282] and is available in either French or English. Though the site is not expressly a newspaper, it does have a link for news and a calendar of current events, and it also provides a portal to all the services supported by the government. The site is clearly intended to be a one-stop resource for every information need of either a visitor or a resident.

Israel, as a democracy, also supports a robust public notice archive on the web,[283] including a posting of recently declassified materials.[284] The government also supports an extensive site for international exporting that provides up-to-date information on bidding opportunities.[285] Tens of thousands of notices are available from categories that include agriculture, construction, energy, the environment, health and public services, industry, information technology, and transportation.

Costs Compared

Among these four models, then, how do the costs of providing public notice compare? By and large, the cost up to the point of posting or publishing is going to remain the same no matter which presentation format is selected. Below are the usual talking points when discussion turns to a preference for web posting rather than traditional newspaper publication of public notice.

- *Costs will be lowered for web posting because publication will not be done by a separate, non-agency private business that charges for publication.*

Publishing a notice involves several steps. The government agency staff preparation of public notices requires a set amount of work that is usually done by the agency required to post the notices rather than by a private publisher. That work is a cost that will exist for an agency as long as there is any requirement for public notices, and therefore a cost to the government.

If the notice then goes directly onto the web, or is sent to a publisher, there is little difference in the cost of notice preparation in a world of digital word processing. If that text must be prepared in some format that presents a difficulty, then an increase in staff time to prepare a notice for upload to a server might in fact lead to higher costs. The details here matter, so generalization is pretty difficult, but generally speaking the preparation of a public notice for distribution is an in-agency cost, not a part of the publisher itemization.

What remains of the cost for publishing notices beyond the government agency office is that of actual distribution, in this case publication.

- *There will be less cost in publishing the notices.*

The cost of publishing in paper-based newspapers is often closely regulated by government statute and relatively easy to know, because bills are submitted to the agency that is required to post the notice. For centuries the expectation has been that the ad rate charged by the newspapers, specifically designated for public notices by the legislature, is recompense for the publishing. Publishing, however, means not only including the notice in the publishing product as requested, but assuring that it is accurately represented and published in accordance with the timetable set up by law.

Often neglected in the cost equation are a number of peripheral expenses to the publisher. Among them is the requirement that the publisher maintain a copy of the publication for future use either by the courts or by citizens who want to know that what is claimed to have been posted was in fact published. And the publisher must maintain a system to verify subscribership so that observers can gauge actual exposure to the publication.

While these are costs subsumed by publishers as part of their business obligations, they represent services that the government and the public at large have long taken for granted. All in all, the publisher is paid at a rate set by the legislature and is required to publish, accurately and on time, a notice that will be kept as a legal record retrieved on request and distributed to a verifiable set of subscribers.

The challenge of providing sustainable records in the digital world has been enormous and is taken seriously by the newspaper industry. After more than a decade of experimenting with a variety of solutions, the news industry was offered a set of guidelines through a consortium effort because "Digital newspaper collections are a key historical record of human activities."[286]

The guidelines provided a template for news collection at various stages of digitization and size. A 50-page guide included sections on inventorying, format management, creation and acquisition, preservation management, partners and permissions, distribution and backup, changes, monitoring, and recovery. Clearly this digital archiving is a complicated and costly "free" service that is part of the public notice contract from which government benefits when paying a news organization for announcement posting.

As governments and activists question the cost of publishing in newspapers, researchers find that pulling all those bills together within a city or state where there are dozens and dozens of agencies has proven to be difficult. It has been estimated that smaller jurisdictions in the United States, for example, might spend $20,000 a year on public notices, while larger cities might spend $500,000.[287] In 2009, the federal government considered posting its judicial forfeiture notices online rather than in newspapers, and the estimated savings was said to be $6.7 million over a five-year period.[288] An explanation of how this savings was estimated was not part of the news report. It is safely assumed, though, that the costs were predicated on previous years' ad rates and probably did not consider separately the expense for web posting that would be required for either government subsidy of a server[289] or the site of the auction house aiding in the sales.[290] Not only were the attendant server or auctioneer costs not calculated, but there also seemed to be no concern about the accountability, accuracy, or timeliness of the posting, or the subsequent maintenance of public records, all part of the previously incurred costs borne by a newspaper ad rate.

- *Web distribution by its very nature will be more inclusive because it is wider, and so fewer publications will be necessary.*

There is no doubt that web posting has the potential of global reach. The web, available through wireless and satellite connectivity, can be accessed anywhere on the planet. WikiLeaks and subsequent national debates, national emergency alerts, and international aid responses were all possible because of the communication networks available through the web.

Public notice, however, is not just about communication. It has been relied on effectively across many centuries because the information contained in an announcement is not just available, but because it is pushed to those who might have use for it. The founders of both the early republics and modern democracies were certain enough that citizens needed to be prompted into learning about what government was doing that they devised ways of putting reports in the way of casual reading.

Legislatures didn't just keep records; copies were sent to each jurisdiction, and reports were carried in hometown newspapers or posted in town squares. In these ways it was hoped that even residents of the most remote areas could happen upon information about government activity. The organizers believed that the difference between citizens seeking information from a central repository, and instead finding the information almost (if not literally) delivered to one's door, is the difference between wondering about what government might be doing and knowing what it is doing. This difference, they thought, would be the success of a republic made up of engaged citizens rather than passive bystanders.

- *Response from the public will be more robust because of the wider distribution of web posting.*

A long-standing political axiom is that everyone might have something to say, but not everyone has something to say that is worth hearing. The same might be said of modern-day web communication. Everyone can post on the web, but not everything posted on the web is worth reading.

Perhaps even harder for modern day political activists, as the web becomes more crowded with posts and clogged with information, is knowing where to look and how to find those things that might be important. The benefits of global reach can quickly be overtaken by a glut of accessible information and a lack of selection tools to sort out what is worthwhile from all that arrives on our computer screens.

As communication systems enjoy wider penetration around the world, citizens who want to participate thoughtfully find it more and more difficult to know which information sources to trust and how best to help themselves to information worth having.

- *There will be no cost to archive the announcements because server space is cheap.*

Public notices that serve a legal function of notification are occasionally referenced in court petitions and are sometimes included as court documents for case records. The fact that the notice was posted or placed according to law, that the contents included specific relevant facts, and that the posting was publicly available are all elements that require a certain consistency in the public notice or legal notice storage and retrieval systems. News organizations that have been designated legal newspapers or newspapers of record win that designation in part because they have a preservation system in place for just these sorts of legal recollection.

For centuries newspapers retained back copies, or bound volumes, of the newspapers, and many publishers chose to move those archival issues into a format such as microfilm, or even microdots. But there were problems with microfilm. For example, sometimes the photographing was sloppy, fuzzy, or low contrast, or portions of the paper were missed. Sometimes the film itself was damaged beyond repair by poor handling or defective reading machinery. Microfilm readers also put a layer of equipment between the viewer and the original publication. Sometimes the machine readers inhibited or changed the way public notices were perceived, creating an experience at variance with the original publication.

Maintaining the microfilm and reader equipment was always expensive, and in the early twenty-first century seemed archaic in an age when digital archives were flourishing. Those responsible for these kinds of records were often glad to migrate away from microfilm and toward digital archives.

Newspapers were not the only organizations to grapple with the migration of records from paper to microfilm to digital archives. Librarians in all areas of guardianship were often on the front lines of discussions and experiments to figure out how best to store, retrieve, and recover records. Many government offices, too, were burdened with huge warehouses of document records that needed to be maintained and made easily accessible. Because so many of the records generated were originally in digital form, it seemed natural to many data clerks that digital archives were the best and easiest way to store the files they had generated.

Management of digital records, in fact, has been a central concern of librarians and computer scientists for at least half a century.[291] It comes as no surprise, then, that there are a variety of systems that can be adopted and a range of solutions that have already been discarded.[292] News librarians debate the costs of paper versus microfilm versus digital almost daily. Note, for example, this exchange from mid-year 2013.

> With an eye to the budget, the debate at my paper is whether or not to continue binding and microfilming our newspaper.
>
> We have a digital content managing system that archives our PDFs (as well as full text and photos) for the past 9 years, and we have a digitized archive for our historic archives where our scanned microfilm collection is fully searchable.
>
> Is there still an argument to be made to either bind or microfilm papers?
>
> I know that long-term preservation of digital born records is still an issue, but I am at a loss how or even if to explain to my bosses that a B&W microfilm copy is "superior" to a color PDF from a preservation perspective, and as such worth the expense. Let alone a bound volume, as newspaper stock has a short preservation span....

> I don't know enough about long-term digital preservation to be able to come up with a plan, nor do we have IT staff knowledgeable enough to assist with this.
>
> Does anybody out there still bind/microfilm? If so, why?[293]

And here is a partial quote from one response that outlines reasons for continuing to maintain microfilm and paper copies of the published issues.

> We still microfilm our newspaper and have no plans to discontinue it. Some reasons why....
>
> * Microfilm lasts for hundreds of years. It's an established archival medium.
>
> * It takes very little physical space to store the complete run of the paper.
>
> * It's a cost-effective way to preserve our newspaper and make it accessible.
>
> * All you need is a light source and magnification to read it (no expensive system upgrades).
>
> * Many area libraries subscribe to our paper on microfilm (revenue for us).
>
> * It shows an exact representation of *The Dispatch* as it was published (nobody can easily alter it, like you can a digital product).
>
> * It is the legal publication of record. (When we get a subpoena, we send a microfilm printout of what we published, which cannot be altered.)
>
> * The Library of Congress requires *The Dispatch* in microfilm format (archival silver halide) for our copyright registration.
>
> * It's an inexpensive "backup" of your publication, in case other archives/formats are compromised.
>
> * Who knows if PDF will continue to be a viable format for page preservation?
>
> * The film is deposited off-site at the Library of Congress for preservation. Off-site storage is essential for peace of mind in case of a catastrophe.

The librarian went on to detail why paper copies may best serve the historical record.

> We stopped "binding" our hard copies in 2004 but continue to save hard copies—unbound—in archival boxes. There was a significant cost savings.

However, we still felt it was important to save hard copies. We found a new solution, instead of paying to bind them (which also sometimes was done too tightly in the margins, which caused problems when we pulled out volumes for scanning historic pages).

The solution was to purchase archival-quality storage boxes for each month of the paper, store the daily papers flat in the boxes, and ship them on a regular basis to offsite secure storage.

Some reasons for saving hard copies:

* Although we still have a cost involved (purchasing the archival storage boxes), and then paying to store them offsite, it is far less than what binding used to cost.

* It is a relatively inexpensive backup of your newspaper.

* If you have been binding papers for decades, it continues that collection.

* If you discover a missing page or entire section in your microfilm, even years later you can go back to the original and have it filmed.

* PDF archives are often incomplete.

* We don't know what technology may be invented to digitize newspapers in the future. Maybe the hard copy would be the best, cheapest or most pristine way to get a digital project done.[294]

There was no one-size-fits-all solution offered among the answers provided, but clearly archiving in any format is a significant enough cost that it cannot be considered "free."

While server space is sometimes said to be a very inexpensive filing cabinet, it is not worry-free. For example, servers require dependable electrical power both to operate and to maintain. Current, light, and cooling can be very expensive. Servers need regular management servicing and repair detection. That labor and the knowledge required to provide the service are usually not cheap.

There are issues of access and organization that are only just becoming evident as users face an array of changes in hardware and software that seem to occur almost daily.[295] None of these improvements is without significant cost. It seems, then, that each format, or platform, has its own problems and expenses, making this aspect of public record publication crucial. Yet it is often ill considered in arguments about legal notice issues.

Conclusions

The cost of public notice is borne in a number of ways, as is evident in the examples above. Government and commerce are the obvious deep pockets that pay the bills, but how the itemization is made within the billing systems determines some of the often-overlooked costs. The value of public notices was discussed in Chapter 2 of this book, and those social tenets need to be carefully balanced, no matter the government form, in any discussion about the costs of providing announcements about government activities. The merits of public information made known through public notice include:

- accessibility to public information,
- accuracy and authenticity of public information,
- social ownership in what public information reports or contains,
- efficiency in social activities made known through public information.

These benefits should be considered when government and constituents navigate the budget and itemization of costs for providing public notice in any format and through any platform. The costs shouldered by government to provide reports and alerts about what it is doing on behalf of constituents should not be considered money that is wasted. It should be seen, and through the centuries of republican government has been seen, as money well spent if it keeps bureaucrats honest and motivates citizens to engage in self-governance.

· 6 ·

PUBLIC NOTICE IN CHANGING ENVIRONMENTS

Public notices as legal and social constructs are part of the political fabric of many nations. Earlier chapters of this book provided numerous examples of both contemporary public notices and some from centuries ago that were posted as legal advertisements or straightforward announcements about personal and social events. These examples demonstrate how public notice has been used to alert and inform citizens about government activity that is either about to happen or that has already begun.

The central function and value of public notices within a representative democracy has been a matter of importance and substance for centuries. Representative democracies cannot fully function unless the public is sufficiently informed about government activities to participate in shaping social issues and engaging with governance decisions. Public notices have served as a workable means of distributing both information and forewarnings of government initiatives for centuries. It should be clear, then, that both the need for and the use of public notices is not a debatable issue. The issue instead is how to most effectively organize, present, distribute, and archive them.

Content and Delivery

For hundreds of years, public notices were delivered verbally by messengers and town criers. But more permanent versions of these important missives could also be found in written form on stone tablets, mountainsides, and obelisks, as well as in the houses of scribes and the halls of public libraries. After the development of movable type and pulp printing sheets in the fifteenth century, public notices were more easily and frequently published in paper form as part of newspapers or posters tacked up in convenient public locations.

Figure 6.1 Public Notice posted on trees in a park along the main thoroughfare of Banja Luka, Bosnia-Herzegovina, 1999. Photo by Shannon E. Martin.

Now, with the seismic changes in communication forms and systems that have developed since the turn of the present century, there is good reason to question the ways in which something so fundamental as public notice must also change. Some governments, organizations, and individuals have already taken to posting legal notices and public announcements on the web for the entire world to see. Others are more cautiously concerned about the availability and temporal qualities of web posting, and so more guardedly continue in the traditional notice systems. How can contemporary society best meet the many requirements of public notice? Answering that question is the purpose of this work.

Throughout this book the author has referred to public notice using various terms—legal notice, legal advertising, special notice, and public announcements. The reason for the variations is, of course, that not all social organizations referred to the same concept using the same nouns. Another way in which the author differentiated various types of public notice was to indicate whether the notice was primarily a social notification or if it was likely meant to meet the more strictly enforced legal notification requirements of a particular political entity.

The multitude of ways of naming legal advertisements and public notice might lead one to infer that though these announcements are central to the health of a representative democracy, they also serve a range of functions. As outlined in Chapter 3, which details legal definitions of public notices, there are many requirements for meeting the demands of courts and legislatures for these announcements. They include not only what should be contained in particular postings, but how the announcements should look, how long they are to remain published, or how frequently they should recur. Even the cost and verification that publication actually took place are often part of the legal mandates.

The social public notices, which are less exacting, are much more loosely constructed to meet the requirements of general announcement and broad publicity. The necessity for speed, permanence, or regularity often differs vastly from its counterpart in the legal advertisement and therefore requires different sorts of communication templates.

This chapter will first present some specific solutions for legal and social notices and then compare these solutions with those that already exist in various places on the web. These remedies are intended to be immediate and practical, though they will not be applicable to all public notice situations.

The remainder of the chapter will be devoted to broader issues and larger solutions that should be effective across many iterations of public notice environments and uses. At the conclusion of the chapter, the author will present a decision tree and a set of thought experiments to help those who are responsible for public notice guidelines and development. The hope, of course, is to create an environment of effective public notices that will lead to a better international congress.

Throughout our examination of public notices there has been a group of variables lurking in every situation. We have been interested in the content of the notice—about what the notice concerns. We have also paid attention to the delivery of the notice—about how it got from the initiator to the recipient. Another of the elements we noted was the source of the notice, and we sometimes remarked on who the recipient of the notice might be, or whether it required some sort of response from the recipient. All of these observations worked to provide us with as many elements for consideration of best practices in public notice that we could find. We have also noted among the many examples that sometimes the systems in place have not worked very well.

What we are ultimately after in all this detail is to identify the most effective public notice system so that representative democracies work as well as possible. If the intention of public notice is to be sure that as many constituents are included in the conveyance of government activities as possible, that means we need to identify how best to get government information to those who need it, even if that need seems to be not much more than a general desire for government information.

Specific Public Notice Situations

Effective public notice will be built on the satisfaction of all of the elements we are investigating—content and delivery, sender and recipient. In order to discover the best solution for any given public notice situation, it may be helpful to work through a series of questions that identify the particular aspects of each circumstance.

For example:

- It is important in public notice to identify who is affected by the information. Is it the general public or an individual? Is it an identifiable segment of the population or a private industry? Are those affected by the information likely to self-identify as needing it, or must they be alerted to the importance of the posted content?
- Another focal question for public notice effectiveness is to ask about who is providing the information. Is it a government agency or an interested private party? Is the information something routinely provided by the agent, or is it specially ordered or prepared for specific purposes?
- Central to effective public notice is the means of communicating the post. Does this agency or private party have limited systems available for providing information? Does the communication require pushing it to the addressee, or can the posting agent rely on constituents pulling the information from a resource within their grasp?

- Another key question to ask is whether a response is required from the recipient. Is the notice necessary simply as a point of reference, or does someone need to let the posting agent know that the information has been received? Essential, too, is the concern about resulting action. Will the government be taking steps on behalf of all citizens, or is there time for constituents to take part in decision making?
- A further concern in some public notice circumstances is whether the announcement has been made in a reliably fixed format that will meet evidence requirements about publication. In some situations courts rely on the archiving of public notices to ensure that the intentions of public notice publication are maintained. This way, when the courts call for evidence of publication and notification, the following questions can be answered: Was the announcement presented as required by law? Was it published as required by law? Is there reason to believe these requirements support the intentions of public notice so that all efforts made serve the best practices of informing the public?

The answers to each of these questions will create a decision tree useful in a range of public notice situations. The outcome of our efforts should determine when the content of a particular notice needs to be pushed directly and unequivocally into the hands of and before the eyes of the addressee by whatever means is best within the public system at hand. Or, the product of the answers to each question may instead indicate when it is good enough to act as if all who need to know whatever is contained in a particular public notice have it at their disposal. In short, all public notices are not equally important to all constituents at all times. The determination of importance is relative to a number of attributes, and our decision tree should help us get to the most effective public notice system we can devise in the constantly changing communication environment in which we find ourselves today.

Legal Notice and Individuals

Chapter 3 of this book focused on legal definitions of public notice and provided a number of examples wherein notification, sometimes called legal notice, was intended for particular recipients.

For example, public notice is used as the government's last recourse for reaching individuals who owe taxes or who are the subject of a lawsuit, and who have not responded to postal notification or could not be located for subpoenas.

In these situations the answers to the questions noted earlier are pretty straightforward. An identifiable individual needs the information, and a government agency is attempting to provide it. A response is required, and action will result. In these particular circumstances a "push" communication mechanism is often required by law. Subpoenas are issued. Court orders are delivered by the police to the door of the individual named in the order. Papers are served directly to the person named in the orders, and certification declares that the task was done by protocols set by the court. In short, the burden of effectively pushing information to concerned parties rests with the government, and little is required of the addressee other than valid identification for receiving the information and the ability to adequately refer to the contents of the notification.

Figure 6.2 Maine Public Notices, July 29, 2013.

In many countries, the necessary protocols are in place to ensure that the content of these kinds of notices is put into the hands of those most concerned with the activity at issue. It is when these systems of individual notification fail that public notice by means of publication is deemed a serviceable remedy. The objection that many governments now hear is that newspaper publication of public notices, when other means have failed, is a waste of taxpayers' money. No one, it has been said, sees these notices, let alone reads them in the newspapers. The money, some argue, could be better spent posting these notices on government-owned online servers, because so many citizens today are more likely to see news items on the web.

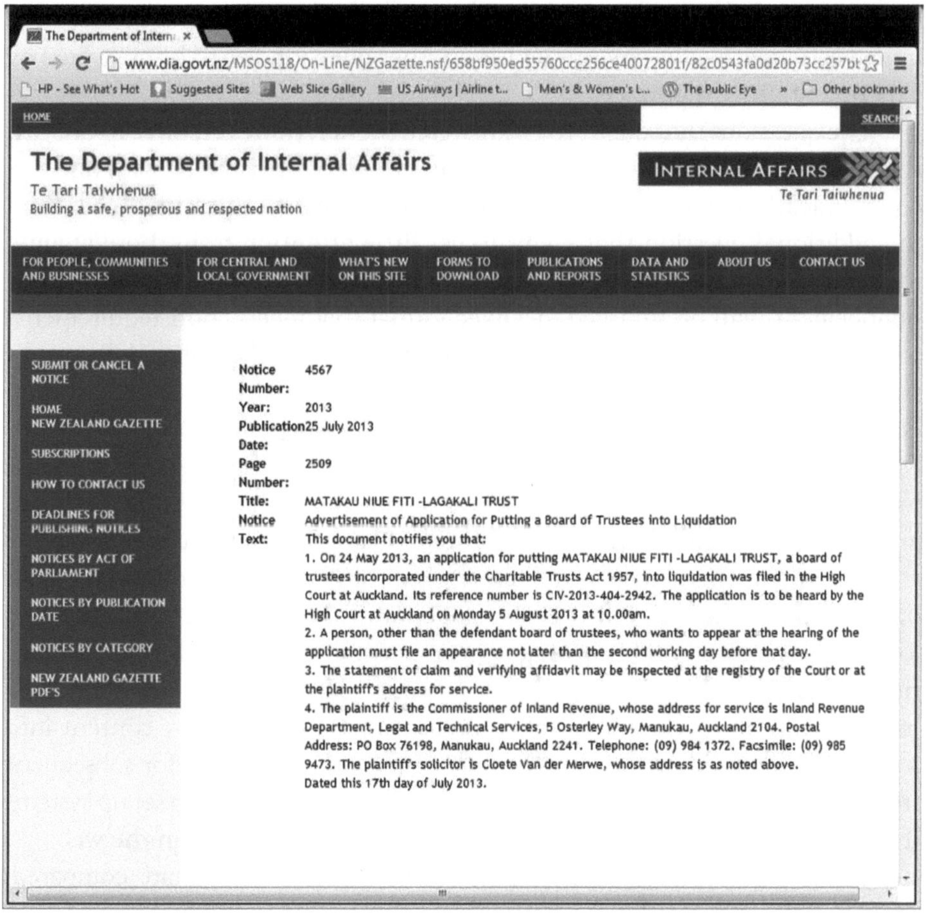

Figure 6.3 Department of Internal Affairs, July 25, 2013, New Zealand.

This rationale seems to miss the original point made by early advocates for ending the practice of newspaper publication. If specific notices are unlikely to be found or read in newspapers in which there are a finite number of pages to peruse each day, what is the likelihood that anyone who needs to see a public notice is likely to discover it among the seemingly infinite number of webpages that exist?

Many newspapers have taken the argument somewhat seriously, though, and now post the public notices submitted to their paper edition on the enhanced web versions of their news publication. Others have organized a statewide or regional online public notice website so that one location can be consulted for a range of announcements. Whether online public notification is any more effective now than newsprint newspaper announcements have been is a question yet to be answered. Whether web-based public notice is more cost-effective for government is another question yet to be answered by experiment and experience.

The questions that ought to be answered sooner, however, have to do with the specific content of a particular notice, to whom it is addressed, and the communication systems available to the government entity involved. And the additional question that seems to get little attention from those arguing for expanded web publication of public notices is whether these online announcements will be archived in a fixed format that meets court requirements when litigation requires notification to be made. When the police deliver subpoenas or clerks hand court orders to litigants, the trail and process are well documented. When notice is made online, the trail is clear only to a point. Most systems of online delivery are no better now than they were 20 years ago when the infamous *New Yorker* cartoon of two dogs at a computer keyboard and screen commented that "On the Internet, nobody knows you're a dog."[296]

Not only is there little assurance of who is, in fact, on the other end of an online communication, but it is also uncertain how the contents of messages look to the receiver, and how that appearance may change with the reformatting of screen preferences or software updates. Though PDFs are often used in an attempt to fix the format of content, it is still easy to copy content into a new document, alter the content, and re-fix to PDF formats for subsequent storage and viewing. For these reasons it is still an arduous task to set up systems that ensure consistency from creation to storage of documents on the web.

As these systems of presentation, delivery, and archiving are compared, the questions that need to be answered in the case of individual notification of public notices are these:

- Is the public notice originating from a government agency and prescribed by law?
- How directly does the notification system deliver content to the individual who needs the notice?
- Is the delivery system the most efficient one available to the agency required to provide notice?
- How firmly is the message content affixed to format, date, and time of issuance, and to delivery presentation?
- If the individual needs to respond to the message content, is the notice verifiable in the form delivered?
- Will there be a need to refer to or recall the information contained in the announcement?
- Is the notification archived and accessible in the form in which it was both issued and delivered?

Today the answers to these questions often suggest that individual notification of legal announcements is not yet ready for online delivery systems. As these systems are developed, though, they well may serve more effectively as legal notice publishers. But until then, they do not seem to replace even the most basic newspaper publication as it now functions. Newsprint newspaper publication still provides fixed format and date archiving, with the assurances of circulation validation, including the web versions often associated with newsprint publishing. It also provides a clear trail of production, publication, delivery, and archiving systems that assure courts of those public notice intentions most often detailed in prescribed legal processing.

Legal Notice and a Class or Group of Individuals

Again, as noted in an earlier chapter, there are times when government agencies must provide information to a group of people who need to know about something the government is about to do or has recently done. This might be a modification to a neighborhood easement or changes to the laws concerning land use. The usual first effort of sending postal notification to landowners within the neighborhood does not always succeed in reaching those who might be affected by the proposed or ongoing government activity—renters, for example, or those responsible for property but not listed as owners. In these kinds of cases, the law and social goodwill suggest broader publication of the public announcement.

Physically posting along public thoroughfares may indeed catch the eye of some residents. This is sometimes being replaced by posting notification on the local websites hosted by government agencies either *ad hoc* or at intervals designated by the agency to serve its timetable. This requires that interested community members access those websites and pull the information onto their desktops without prompting and without expectation that something of interest will be found.

Some communities are also pushing notification to those with email addresses by sending notices directly to community members who subscribe to a listserv, or automatic group emailing service. This requires that interested group members proactively subscribe themselves at an appropriate time in order to receive the notification.

But another means of broadcasting the neighborhood information may be publication in a local or legally designated newspaper of record. This method has the appeal of providing the information to anyone who might be interested, whether or not they reside in or own property in the affected geographic area. It also has the added benefit of spreading the information of the notice more effectively by word of mouth rather than direct government action.

As was noted in Chapter 4, there is a wide range of Internet user saturation, varying from zero to 100% of a country's population. Until the number of savvy Internet users constitute a majority of a community's residents, it would seem foolish to rely on web postings and email for active engagement in community affairs. Even in a community of 100% Internet users, the records of government activities need to be archived in a format that is unalterable in the face of controversy, and accessible to the least experienced. For many communities that means retaining paper records. Though digital records often require little space for storage, they still require complicated systems of hardware and software to archive, organize, retrieve, read, and distribute. Paper, on the other hand, requires no more than the space to shelve, some protection from extreme heat, and the skill of literacy to read.

Public Notice and Entire Communities

The most common examples of public notices across all the circumstances reported in this book are situations in which government needs to provide every member of the community with information about what it has been doing or is about to do. These include announcements about upcoming meetings or law enforcement, bureaucratic appointments or agency reports, proposed budgets or project expenditures—in other words, activities that affect all members of the community in some way. These sorts of announcements are sometimes required by specific laws; at other times the government thinks that publication of community-relevant information is prudent.

In all of these cases, though, accessible content and wide distribution ought to be the aim, preferably in formats that are usable to both the government and the constituents. The fact that the reports or proposals or appointments have been made public begs the question of whether all community members will attend to the usefulness of the announcement, but in every case there are some who are glad to know what government is up to on their behalf.

The key elements in this general circumstance have more to do with the uncomplicated presentation of content and the accessibility of the content. So, the questions that need to be answered are these:

- Is the public notice originating from a government agency and prescribed by law?
- How broadly does the notification system deliver content to all community members?
- Is the delivery system the most efficient one available to the agency required to provide notice?
- Is the delivery system the most easily available one to the least experienced of the community members?
- If community members want to respond to the message content, is the notice verifiable in the form delivered?
- Will there be a need to refer to or recall the information contained in the announcement?
- Is the notification archived and accessible in the form in which it was both issued and delivered?

The earlier sets of questions focused on the targeted distribution of information and the timeliness of that distribution. This series of questions is tailored to the concerns of population inclusion and record stability. The greater the social media literacy among community members, then the higher the likelihood that successful public notice can be achieved through web access. But government must continue to be thoughtful about what means of communication best suits the entire population, and where newspapers and radio are still the media of choice, government is wisest in formatting its announcements for those platforms.

Public Notice and Society

Announcements made by individuals, community groups, or private industry and broadcast to anyone interested hold a different sort of place in our attention. Though most of the examples in the previous chapters have been about government, there have been a number of instances in which someone simply wanted to make some news known to anyone who might wish to know about that news. These often were a social "heads up" that did not carry the force of government or a legal system, but were meant as a good-neighbor warning, or glad tidings.

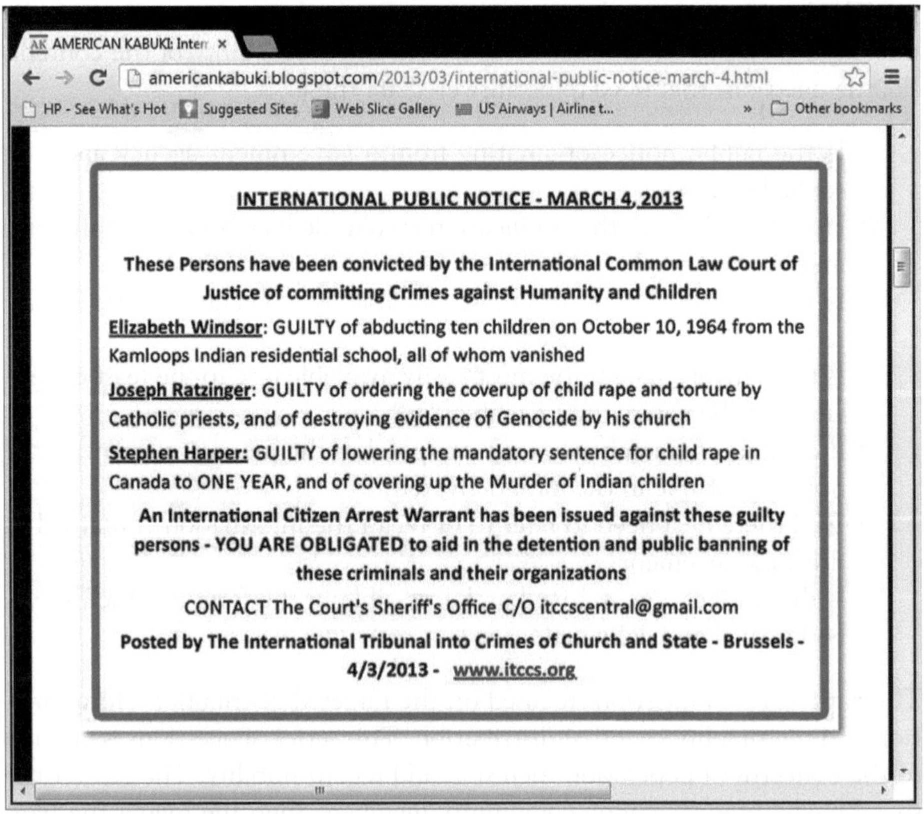

INTERNATIONAL PUBLIC NOTICE - MARCH 4, 2013

These Persons have been convicted by the International Common Law Court of Justice of committing Crimes against Humanity and Children

Elizabeth Windsor: GUILTY of abducting ten children on October 10, 1964 from the Kamloops Indian residential school, all of whom vanished

Joseph Ratzinger: GUILTY of ordering the coverup of child rape and torture by Catholic priests, and of destroying evidence of Genocide by his church

Stephen Harper: GUILTY of lowering the mandatory sentence for child rape in Canada to ONE YEAR, and of covering up the Murder of Indian children

An International Citizen Arrest Warrant has been issued against these guilty persons - YOU ARE OBLIGATED to aid in the detention and public banning of these criminals and their organizations

CONTACT The Court's Sheriff's Office C/O itccscentral@gmail.com

Posted by The International Tribunal into Crimes of Church and State - Brussels - 4/3/2013 - www.itccs.org

Figure 6.4 "These Persons have been convicted by the International Common Law Court of Justice of committing Crimes against Humanity and Children," March 3, 2013.

In most of these sorts of illustrations reported herein, the headline "Public Notice" was included by the announcement's creator with the intention of looking like something that implied enforcement. For example, the announcement "Public Notice: These parking spaces are for customers of this store" is often unenforceable if the parking spaces are on a street that is a city thoroughfare. But the intention of including the phrase "Public Notice" is to lend an air of authority to the desires of the shop owner. Similarly, if someone posts a notice on the Internet disavowing any affiliation with another person or group, it is hardly worth more than simply alerting everyone who comes across the announcement to be warned off of an assumption.

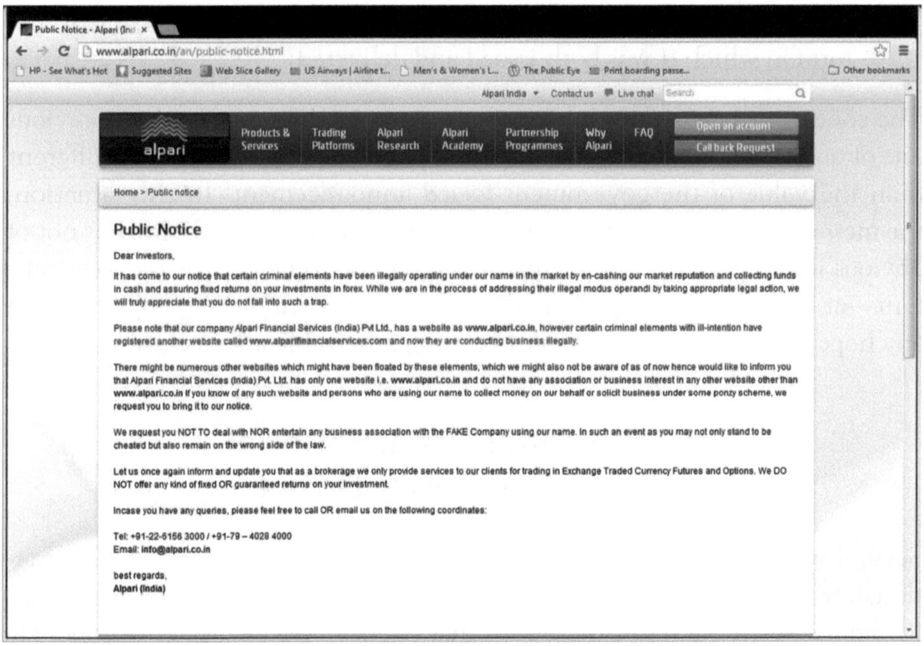

Figure 6.5 Alpari Financial Services Warning.

If it is understood that public notices within social contexts are nothing more than friendly—or not so friendly—warnings, then the content and distribution are relatively simple matters to determine. The questions to be answered are these:

- Is the public notice originating from an individual, a social group, or a private industry?
- How broadly does the notification need to be delivered in order to reach all intended community members?

- Is the delivery system the most efficient one available for these purposes?
- Is the content of the message clear enough to be understood by all the intended recipients?
- Is the delivery system the one most easily available to the least experienced of the community members?
- If community members want to respond to the message content, is the notice verifiable in the form delivered?
- Will there be a need to refer to or recall the information contained in the announcement?
- Is there a need for the notification to be archived and accessible in the form in which it was both issued and delivered?

The concerns expressed in this set of questions are different than our previous sets of questions because the value of the public notice is somewhat different than the value of the government-issued announcement. In this situation, the message is intended for informal enforcement of a social desire, but not of obvious legal standing. The recipient can choose to ignore the message content—at his or her social peril, perhaps—but if the announcement is to have any hope of being effective, it must be comprehensible and accessible.

International, Transnational, and Global Public Notice

Several websites recently began hosting pages claiming to provide international, transnational, or global public notice. However, there were some sharp variations in the claims of these sites that ought to lead a viewer to conclude that there is not a universal understanding of the purposes of public notice.

For example, one site claimed to contain not only all government announcements but also news stories about government activity. Another site offered to post any notice that the originator wanted to have seen by the world and promised no editing or censorship of any kind. Some sites charged small fees, while others posted for free but appeared to rely on advertisements or the support of a sponsoring organization to keep the sites alive and active. Among these sites there was no apparent effort to identify whether the site was available to particular countries, regions, or all nations. There was also no indication that the particular sites were in fact viewable in all countries, or if instead they were catering to a region of the world or a class of nations.

The need for transnational public notice requires little imagination. It is easy to find governments posting legal notices that were clearly intended for citizens who were non-residents of the source country. There were several instances among the examples in Chapter 4 that obviously were announcements aimed at companies and foreign nationals who might want to do business in the posting country. And there were other examples where individuals with legal liability concerns were trying to reach outside their home country to shed their responsibilities for others' bad acts. These efforts suggest that there is indeed a market for public notice that stretches beyond domestic borders.

The need is not an invention of the Internet, nor even a new activity. Newspapers that were published for international audiences often carried legal advertisements or public notices of the very sort found on the web today. In fact, those newspapers that once carried the announcements still publish them. The expectation was that since the newspaper was so portable and intended for international readership, it was the best and only practical placement vehicle if governments, businesses, or individuals needed to circulate legal notices outside domestic readership.

Figure 6.6. "UL Warns of counterfeit UL Mark on power adapter."

The intention of these notices was to be certain that anyone outside the country with an interest in the transnational news found in the paper's pages would see the advertisement and know the context of the announcement—date and place of origin. The viewer of the newspaper's notices was reasonably confident that the advertisement had been placed intentionally and that the newspaper provided some authority if the contents of the announcement were called into question. This is not to say that the newspaper vetted the agent placing the notice, but that the notice was at least identically presented in every issue of the publication. Everyone who saw that day's newspaper, whenever or wherever they read it, saw the same content in the advertisement.

For many years the best distribution that could be hoped for by anyone posting a legal notice in the newspaper was a transnational or international publishing organization. For example, the *International Herald*, a cooperative news venture for many years between the *Washington Post* and *The New York Times* in Paris, published a daily newspaper in English that was sold across Europe and various other locations around the world. Though the news in each local edition was slightly tailored to that geographic region, the readership was expected to be international. Global reach for such a publication with turn-of-the-twentieth-century technology was beyond the scope of most news organizations.

Today, however, global distribution is closer to a reality. While access and availability are not universal, the prospects are better than ever to at least make news available in real time around the world. By the second decade of the twenty-first century, Twitter and Facebook demonstrated this daily. Not only can an entire country's population know what is happening within its borders, but everyone anywhere in the world with an interest in the nation's business can be viewing the same government announcements and public pronouncements.

The question, then, for those interested in wider distribution of public notice is to determine what the purpose and the value of such wide publication of public announcements is or ought to be. The following questions might be useful in determining whether Internet posting of public notice for global distribution is worth pursuing.

- Is the public notice originating from a government agency, and is transnational publication of the announcement prescribed by law?
- Or is the public notice emanating from an individual, a social group, or a private industry with a desire for transnational publication?
- If the notice is required by law to be published transnationally, then who is the enforcing agent to ensure that the requirements have been met?

- How broadly does the notification system deliver public notice content to all countries?
- Is the delivery system the most efficient one available to the agency, industry, social group, or individual desiring or required to provide notice?
- Is the delivery system the most easily available to the least experienced of the country's residents?
- If the country's residents want to respond to the message content, is the notice verifiable for authorship, timeliness, and authority in the form delivered?
- Will there be a need to refer to or recall the information contained in the announcement?
- Is the notification archived and accessible in the form in which it was both issued and delivered?

The opportunities to at least make available a public notice to all who seek it are better now than ever because of the Internet and the World Wide Web. However, the accessibility and authority of any particular posting are more complicated than ever before. While email services may be able to push particular notice content to those who know to ask for it, it is less likely that the broadcast effect of announcements on the web is effective in capturing the attention of those who need to be constantly surfing and pulling content onto their desktops.

The international services, too, that might provide push or pull technology will be opportunistic, and those who receive public notices, or surf in search of them, need to be more vigilant than ever about the sites and postings of these announcements. Viewers need to be ever mindful of the *New Yorker* cartoon as they read transnational, international, and global public notices.

And though language barriers are rapidly falling as many governments adopt English as a second language for commerce, there are still billions of community members around the world who do not speak, read, or understand a widely used language such as English or Chinese. So, even if notices are available, and even if content is pulled up through particular searches, it is still unlikely that any particular announcement will be seen, read, and understood equally around the world.

Conclusions

The effectiveness of public notice cannot be measured by a single norm or set of all-encompassing variables. It must be assessed instead on a group or set of elements. There are many differences, for example, between notice to individuals about individual-relevant concerns, and notice to all who may be concerned about particular government activities. As a result, the appropriate solution to modernizing public notice in each case is as much about attending to the means of distribution as about careful consideration of the importance of particular information to each recipient. In all cases, however, record keeping and archiving are ever-important responsibilities of government. Representative democracies cannot perform effectively if their activities cannot be recalled, reviewed, and revised toward improvement each time there is a change in officeholder.

The work reported here intends to provide examples of success and failure, as well as the context of those situations. The aim is to make it possible for bureaucrats and community members to decide together how they want public information handled. These solutions need to be in place before social activists turn to freedom of access laws, privacy regulations, and free speech provisions to get what they need for collective participation.

The series of questions provided above for particular contexts are not exhaustive and should be expanded as needed. It should be clear, however, that a decision tree or a series of questions and answers will guide democracies toward a better solution than the adoption of one-size-fits-all templates. The initiation of a sequence of questions, then, should be employed to elicit the appropriate solution for public notice now and any time public information requires distribution.

Here, again, are the initial questions for consideration:

- Is the public notice originating from a government agency and prescribed by law, or is it originating from an individual, a social group, or private industry?
- Is the content of the notice time sensitive?
- How directly does the notification system deliver content to the individuals who need the notice?
- Or how broadly does the notification need to be delivered in order to reach all desired community members?
- Is the delivery system the most efficient one available to the agency that is required to provide notice?
- Or is the delivery system the most efficient one available for the purposes of warning affected community members of a social desire?
- Does the notice need to be pushed directly to individuals, or can it instead be left to the individuals to seek out the message content?

- How firmly is the message content affixed to format, date, time of issuance, and delivery presentation?
- If an individual needs to respond to the message content, is the notice verifiable in the form delivered?
- Will there be a need to refer to or recall the information contained in the announcement?
- Is the notification archived and accessible in the form in which it was both issued and delivered?
- Is the archival system accessible to all who might need to recall public information?

Opportunities Rather Than Challenges

The twenty-first century is often characterized as the new age of communication. Social media have reshaped the ways in which individuals share ideas and manage dialogues around the globe. The substance of those conversations ranges from how to tie a bow to how to save the government. Whatever the content of the exchanges may be, the speed and depth of an exchange is chiefly within the control of the senders and receivers.

Now public announcements can be globally distributed or targeted to an individual in ways that seem to answer every kind of communal need. Posting content can be detailed *ad nauseum* or so briefly noted as to be no more than a twitter. WikiLeaks has proven that governments or corporations do not as easily control data content, storage, and distribution as they once did, and many activists see this as a very good thing for the world.

It has been estimated that about 154.6 billion emails are sent daily and that there are more than 1 million blog posts each day. With all that traffic on the global web, might it be useful to have a least a portion of so much communication be about public notices—those long and short announcements about public business necessary to make better decisions about the government that surrounds each of us?

With all the networking that the web provides, might we harness some of that to learn that, let's say, state government in Maine lost money when insurance defaulted on claims in the same way that a provincial government in some faraway country felt the same sort of loss to the same sort of scheme? Or that Harry Smith, who treated his relatives to a bad investment, went on to treat his new friends in other circles on the other side of the world to the same kind of bad investment?

With all the space available on all the servers worldwide, might there be enough room for both the brief and in-depth public notices that serve as warnings, alerts, acknowledgments, listings, and general knowledge about what may affect us? And might there be an algorithm written to help sort and sift, coordinate and connect those items that we need to know before we decide what is best for our communities and ourselves? The value of public notice is indisputable. What we do now to advance that value in an age of rapid communication capacity and growth may well be the mark of human advancement or decline.

A recent case argued before the Chancery Court in Tennessee challenged the sufficiency of a public notice that simply posted the fact that a meeting would be held, and opted to leave out the agenda, which included a controversial review and possible community board approval. The trial court judge questioned whether public notice in the newspaper was ever sufficient, no matter the content, while the appeals court judges found that the newspaper posting requirements had met the legal requirements.[297] The Public Notice Resource Center filed an amicus brief with the appeals court and urged recognition that the notification error was not with the system—in this case community newspaper publication—but with the brevity of the notice. PNRC president Bradley Thompson II, publisher of the *Detroit Legal News*, said of the trial court:

> We were very disturbed by the Chancery Court's implication that if a matter is controversial, you should trust government-owned media to disseminate the public notice. That finding turns the whole idea of public notice upside down. The fact that the Planning Commission usually posted its agenda on its website, but did not do so before the controversial meeting in question should be sufficient evidence that the right way to inform the citizens is through an independent medium. The newspaper has been the trusted vehicle for public notice since the nation's founding. There is no reason to depart from the wisdom of using a newspaper. The problem in this case was that after you read the public notice, you still didn't know enough to decide whether you wanted to get involved.
>
> So the lesson for us was twofold: pick the right vehicle for your notice, and then make the notice worthwhile. The county followed its own tradition in choosing a newspaper, and we think the newspaper is the right vehicle. But it did no more than the law required in forming the content of its notice. That was where the citizens of Tennessee were ill-served. We are urging the court to uphold the county's action and to make a strong suggestion to the legislature that better open meetings notices are needed in the state.

The value of public notice as a means of effective self-governance cannot be overstated. It has been demonstrated throughout this book that the very earliest of representative democracies employed public notice to chronicle government work with an eye toward encouraging community participation in government decision making. In the best of times, everyone benefitted from the contributions of all who were well informed and actively engaged in government's work. At other times, poor public notice practices contributed to social upheaval and led to bureaucratic failure. It is, therefore, the hope of this writer that the work here is not bound by its publication date but finds use wherever and whenever the book is found, in whatever form that might be.

NOTES

1. William T. Bluhm, *Theories of the Political System*, 3rd ed. (London: Prentice-Hall, 1978).
2. The Federalist was a series of 85 essays published in the *New York Packet*, October 1787 through August 1788.
3. P.J. Rhodes, "Public Documents in the Greek States: Archives and Inscriptions," *Greece & Rome* 48, no. 1 (April 2001): 33–44.
4. James P. Sickinger, *Public Records and Archiving in Classical Athens* (Chapel Hill: University of North Carolina Press, 1999), 1.
5. Elizabeth Eisenstein, *The Printing Press as an Agent of Change* (Cambridge: Cambridge University Press, 1979). For an overview of writing and text production see Leila Avrin, *Scribes, Script, and Books: The Book Arts from Antiquity to the Renaissance* (Chicago: American Library Association, 1991).
6. See, for example, House of Lords, "The Report of the Lords Committee to View and Consider the Publick Records," by John Baskett, printer to the King's most excellent majesty (1719); Aimee C. Quinn, "Keeping the Citizenry Informed: Early Congressional Printing and 21st Century Information Policy," *Government Information Quarterly* 20, no. 3 (2003): 281–93.
7. For example, see Joseph Frank, *The Beginnings of the English Newspaper: 1620–1660* (Cambridge, MA: Harvard University Press, 1961); George Boyce, James Curran, and Pauline Wingate, eds., *Newspaper History from the 17th Century to the Present Day* (Beverly Hills, CA: Sage Publications, 1978).
8. See, for example, David A. Copeland, *Debating the Issues in Colonial Newspapers* (Westport, CT: Greenwood Press, 2000); Richard D. Brown, *Knowledge Is Power: The Diffusion of Information*

in Early America, 1700–1865 (New York: Oxford University Press, 1989); Geneva Overholser and Kathleen Hall Jamieson, eds., *The Press* (New York: Oxford University Press, 2005).

9. David Holmes, *Communication Theory: Media, Technology and Society* (Thousand Oaks, CA: Sage, 2005), 10.
10. Holmes, *Communication Theory*, 9.
11. Katrin Voltmer, "The Media, Government Accountability, and Citizen Engagement," in *Public Sentinel: News Media and Governance Reform*, ed. Pippa Norris (Washington, DC: World Bank, 2010), 395.
12. P.D. Driscoll and others, "Public Support for Access to Government Records: A National Survey," in *Access Denied: Freedom of Information in the Information Age*, ed. C.N. Davis and S.L. Splichal (Ames: Iowa State University Press, 2000), 23–36; Suzanne J. Piotrowski and G.G. Van Ryzin, "Citizen Attitudes Toward Transparency in Local Government," *American Review of Public Administration* 37 (2007): 306–323; David Cuillier and Suzanne J. Piotrowski, "Internet Information-Seeking and Its Relation to Support for Access to Government Records," *Government Information Quarterly* 26 (2009): 441–49.
13. Stephen Lax, "The Internet and Democracy," in *Web Studies: Rewiring Media Studies for the Digital Age*, ed. David Gauntlett (Oxford: Oxford University Press, 2000), 160.
14. Madison, James, *Notes of Debates in the Federal Convention of 1787 Reported by James Madison*, Introd. by Adrienne Koch (Athens: Ohio University Press, 1985).
15. George Read, quoting from a letter of John Adams, *Niles' Register* 14, p. 258, no. xvi, July 13, 1818; in William Thompson Read, *Life and Correspondence of George Read* (New York: Lippincott, 1870), 99.
16. U.S. Continental Congress, "Resolution 4," *Extracts from the Votes and Proceedings of the American Continental Congress, Held at Philadelphia, 1774*, published by order of the Congress, Philadelphia, First Group, p. 3.
17. U.S. Continental Congress, Signed by Henry Middleton, President, *Extracts from the Votes and Proceedings of the American Continental Congress, Held at Philadelphia, 1774*, published by order of the Congress, Philadelphia, First Group, 66–71; also in 1774, October 26, *Journals of Congress, Containing the Proceedings, from Sept. 5, 1774 to Jan. 1, 1776*, vol. 1, published by order of Congress Philadelphia, 1776.
18. United States of America, The Declaration of Independence, 1776, lines 109–14.
19. United States of America, Articles of Confederation, 1777, lines 45–47.
20. Articles of Confederation, 1777, lines 205–10.
21. Articles of Confederation, 1777, lines 368, 373–84.
22. Massachusetts Constitution of 1780, art. XVIII.
23. Madison, "Preface," in *Notes of Debates* (1985), 17.
24. Madison, *Notes of Debates*, May 29, p. 28.
25. Madison, *Notes of Debates*, August 11, p. 433.
26. Madison, *Notes of Debates*, August 11, Elbridge Gerry, of Massachusetts, and Roger Sherman, of Connecticut.
27. *Notes of Debates*, August 11, p. 434.
28. *Notes of Debates*, September 14, p. 641.
29. *Notes of Debates*, August 27, pp. 535–40.
30. *Notes of Debates*, August 20, p. 486.

31. *Notes of Debates*, September 12, p. 630.
32. *Notes of Debates*, September 14, p. 640.
33. *Notes of Debates*, September 17, pp. 658–59.
34. *Notes of Debates*, September 17, p. 659.
35. "Letters of a Federal Farmer by R.H. (Richard Henry) Lee," Letter V, October 15, 1787, in *Pamphlets on the Constitution of the United States*, ed. Paul Leicester Ford (Brooklyn, NY: n.p., 1888), 322–23.
36. 2 Eng. Stat. at Large 191 (1341–1411).
37. *Rex v. Fraternity of Hostmen*, 93 Eng. Rep. 1144 (1745).
38. See, for example, *Ferry v. Williams*, 41 N.J.L. 332 (1879); *Clay v. Ballard*, 13 S.E. 262 (Va. 1891); *Cormack v. Wolcott*, 15 P. 245 (Kan. 1887); *Webber v. Townley*, 5 N.W. 971 (Mich. 1880).
39. *State v. King*, 154 Ind. 625 (1900).
40. *Nowack v. Auditor General*, 234 Mich. 203–4 (1928).
41. For a current list see, for example, *The Economist's Democracy Index*, http://www.eiu.com/Handlers/WhitepaperHandler.ashx?fi=Democracy_Index_2011_Updated.pdf&mode=wp&campaignid=DemocracyIndex2011, viewed January 2013; or *Freedom House Reports*, http://www.freedomhouse.org/issues/democratic-governance, viewed January 2013.
42. See, for example, Switzerland Constitution (2000), Articles 16, 17, and 18 among the citizen rights; Articles 45, 55, 92, 93, 136–42, 158, and 169 in government operations.
43. Germany Constitution (2009), Articles 1–19.
44. Switzerland Constitution, Article 17.
45. Germany Constitution (2009), Article 42 (3).
46. Constitution of the Republic of Lithuania, 1992, Chapter 2, The Individual and the State.
47. General Provisions, Law on Provision of Information to the Public, Republic of Lithuania, No. 1–1418, July 2, 1996, as amended by No IX-2176, April 2004, Article 6 and Article 21.
48. *Butterworths New Zealand Law Dictionary*, 4th ed. (Wellington, New Zealand: Butterworths, 1995), 239; and Public Act 1924 No. 11, *Acts Interpretation Act 1924*, (j)(III).
49. Ministry of Business, Innovation and Employment, New Zealand, http://www.business.govt.nz/companies, viewed January 2013.
50. Court of Justice of the European Union (Fourth Chamber), Case C-279/11 heard June 1, 2011 and decided December 19, 2012, pp. 14–17 (#33–36) referencing Regulation 19(2).
51. European Union Council Directive 27 June 1985, 85/377/EEC, Official Journal No. L175, 05/07/1985, p. 0040–0048.
52. For a thorough history of the U.S. National Archives and Records Service, see H.G. Jones, *The Records of a Nation: Their Management, Preservation, and Use* (New York: Atheneum, 1969).
53. See, for example, "Overview of all FOI law around the world, 2011 update, http://www.llrx.com/features/foilawsoverview.htm, viewed January 2013; "FOI Law Spreading Around the World," http://www.wri.org/stories/2010/09/freedom-information-laws-spreading-around-world, viewed January 2013; "Freedom of Information: The right to know," http://unesdoc.unesco.org/images/0019/001936/193653e.pdf, viewed January 2013.
54. For an extensive history of early Anglo-American newspapers and the postmaster system, see Charles E. Clark, *The Public Prints: The Newspaper in Anglo-American Culture* (New York: Oxford University Press, 1994).

55. See, for example, Herbert N. Foerstel, *Freedom of Information and the Right to Know: Origins and Applications of the Freedom of Information Act* (Westport, CT: Greenwood Press, 1999); Shannon E. Martin, *Freedom of Information: The News the Media Use* (New York: Peter Lang, 2008).
56. For an example of current efforts to establish global public notice, see http://www.ul.com/global/por/pages/corporate/newsroom/publicnotices/, or http://www.islamicsolutions.com/about/public-notice/, viewed January 2013.
57. For a list of U.S. state legislatures and courts that have recently initiated legal changes to the publication of public notices so that they appear on the web either exclusively or in conjunction with print publications, see http://watchnotice.wordpress.com/research/, viewed January 2013.
58. See http://watchnotice.wordpress.com/research/, viewed January 2013.
59. See, for example, the public notice consortiums available at http://www.publicnoticeads.com, http://www.mypublicnotices.com/PublicNotice.asp, http://floridapublicnotices.com/, and http://www.ananews.com/wordpress/index.php/public-notices/public-notice-search/
60. Maurice Rickards, *The Public Notice: An Illustrated History* (New York: Clarkson N. Potter, 1973).
61. Rickards, *The Public Notice*, 7–8.
62. *Oxford Dictionary*, http://oxforddictionaries.com/definition/english/public, viewed January 2013.
63. *Oxford Dictionary*, http://oxforddictionaries.com/definition/english/private, viewed January 2013.
64. *Black's Law Dictionary*, centennial ed. (St. Paul, MN: West Publishing, 1991).
65. U.S. Continental Congress, *Extracts from the Votes and Proceedings of the American Continental Congress, Held at Philadelphia, on the Fifth of September, 1774*, published by order of the Congress, Philadelphia (1775). Group 2, 36–37.
66. William Thompson Read, *Life and Correspondence of George Read* (Philadelphia: Lippincott, 1870), 82.
67. John Adams, *History of the Dispute with America from Its Origin in 1754, Written in 1774* (London: J. Stockdale, 1784), 4.
68. Benjamin Franklin, broadside dated July 7, 1803, lower right corner, housed in the Benjamin Franklin Collection, Clements Library, University of Michigan.
69. Article 13 and Article 14, "Protection of Individual Rights and Human Dignity," and "Protection of Privacy," General Provisions, Law on Provision of Information to the Public (2004).
70. Samuel D. Warren and Louis D. Brandeis, "The Right to Privacy," *Harvard Law Review* 4, no. 5 (1890): 193; Anne Wells Branscomb, *Who Owns Information?* (New York: Basic Books, 1994); Harold L. Cross, *The People's Right to Know: Legal Access to Public Records and Proceedings* (New York: Columbia University Press, 1953); James Russell Wiggins, *Freedom or Secrecy* (New York: Oxford University Press, 1956); Ronald Backes, "Freedom, Information, Security," *Seton Hall Constitutional Law Journal* 10 (2000): 927; Michael Hoefges and others, "Privacy Rights Versus FOIA Disclosure Policy: The 'Uses and Effects' Double Standard in Access to Personally-Identifiable Information in Government Records," *William & Mary Bill of Rights Journal* 12, no. 1 (2003): 1; Shannon Martin and

others, "State Laws Requiring World Wide Web Dissemination of Information: A Review of State Government Mandates for Documents Online," *Information and Communication Technology Law* 10 (2001): 167; Francis E. Rourke, "Administrative Secrecy: A Congressional Dilemma," *American Political Science Review* 54 (1960): 684.

71. Wayne Logan, *Knowledge as Power: Criminal Registration and Community Notification Laws in America* (Stanford, CA: Stanford University Press, 2009), 142.
72. Wayne Logan, *Knowledge as Power: Criminal Registration and Community Notification Laws in America* (Stanford, CA: Stanford University Press, 2009), 155.
73. See, for example, http://www.aclu.org/protecting-civil-liberties-digital-age, viewed January 2013; https://www.eff.org/work, viewed January 2013.
74. *See* Peter S. Kozinets, "Access to the E-Mail Records of Public Officials: Safeguarding the Public's Right to Know," *Communications Lawyer* 25 (Summer 2007): 17.
75. "An Act to Provide for the Safe-Keeping of the Act, Records and Seal of the United States, and for Other Purposes," First Congress, Session 1, Chapter XIV, September 15, 1789, p. 68.
76. "An Act to Provide," First Congress, Session 1, Chapter XIV, September 15, 1789, Section 7.
77. U.S. Constitution, Art. II, Sec. 3.
78. 3 *Annals of Congress* 493 (1792).
79. *The Writings of Thomas Jefferson*, ed. Paul Leicester Ford (New York: Putnam, 1904), 3:189.
80. 4 *Annals of Congress* 56 & 250 (1794).
81. George Washington, "The President's Message, on the Treaty Papers," *Centinel-Office* (Boston: Benjamin Russell, April 7, 1796).
82. 8 *Annals of Congress* 1374–5 (1798).
83. Letter to Robert Livingston, in *The Writings of Thomas Jefferson*, ed. Paul Leicester Ford, 8:143–44.
84. Communication from Jefferson to George Hay, in *The Writings of Thomas Jefferson*, ed. Paul Leicester Ford, 9: n. 55–64.
85. *Marbury v. Madison*, 5 U.S. 137 (1803).
86. Shannon E. Martin, *Freedom of Information: The News the Media Use* (New York: Peter Lang, 2008), 44.
87. Memorandum from President Reagan to Heads of Executive Departments and Agencies, "Procedures Governing Responses to Congressional Requests for Information," November 4, 1982.
88. Roger Sherman, *Remarks on a Pamphlet Entitled "A Dissertation on the Political Union and Constitution of the Thirteen United States of North America" by "a Citizen of Philadelphia"* (Philadelphia: T & B Green, 1784).
89. 5 U.S.C. 1002, 60 Stat. 238 (1946).
90. See, for example, Walter Gellhorn, "The Administrative Procedures Act: The Beginnings," *Virginia Law Review* 72, no. 2 (March 1986): 219; Martin Shapiro, "APA: Past, Present, Future," *Virginia Law Review* 72 (1986): 447; Edward Rubin, "It's Time to Make the Administrative Procedures Act Administrative," *Cornell Law Review* 89 (2003): 95.

91. Pub. L. No. 89–487, 80 Stat. 250 (1966).
92. Pub. L. No. 87–579, 76 Stat. 352 (1962).
93. See Shannon E. Martin and Kathleen Hansen, *Newspaper of Record in Digital Age: From Hot Type to Hot Link* (Westport, CT: Praeger, 1998), ch.1, pp. 1–15.
94. Kozinets, "Access to the E-Mail Records," 24.
95. James P. Sickinger, *Public Records and Archives in Classical Athens* (Chapel Hill: University of North Carolina Press, 1999), 14.
96. Sickinger, *Public Records and Archives*, 61.
97. See Lionel Casson, *Libraries in the Ancient World* (New Haven, CT: Yale University Press, 2001), 29.
98. Casson, *Libraries*, 29–30.
99. Casson, *Libraries*, 35.
100. Casson, *Libraries*, 31.
101. Casson, *Libraries*, 34–35.
102. See, for example, Edwin Wolf 2nd, *At the Instance of Benjamin Franklin: A Brief History of the Library Company of Philadelphia, 1731–1976* (Philadelphia, PA: The Library Company of Philadelphia, 1976), 2.
103. John Y. Cole, *Jefferson's Legacy: A Brief History of the Library of Congress* (Washington, DC: Library of Congress, 1993).
104. See, for example, Pennsylvania Constitution, Pa. Const. of 1790, art. I, §14.
105. Massachusetts Constitution of 1780, art. XVIII.
106. Letter from James Madison to W.T. Barry, 4 August 1822, in *The Writings of James Madison*, ed. Gaillard Hunt (New York: G.P. Putnam's Sons, 1910), 9:103. ("A popular Government, without popular information, or the means of acquiring it, is but a Prologue to a Farce or a Tragedy; or, perhaps both. Knowledge will forever govern ignorance: And a people who mean to be their own Governors, must arm themselves with the power which knowledge gives.")
107. Susan Lee Grabler, "Government Information of, by, and for the People: The Changing Mission of the American Library Association's Public Documents Committee, 1876–1956," *Journal of Government Information* 22, no. 1 (1995): 45–46.
108. Elizabeth G. McPherson, "The Southern States and the Reporting of Senate Debates, 1789–1802," *Journal of Southern History* 12, no. 2 (1946): 223–25.
109. See, for example, American Association of Law Libraries, State-By-State Report on Authentication of Online Legal Resources (2007), available at http://www.aallnet.org/aallwash/authen_rprt/authenfinalreport.pdf; Kelly Kunsch, "Diogenes Wanders the Superhighway: A Proposal for Authentication of Publicly Disseminated Documents on the Internet," *Seattle University Law Review* 20 (1997): 749.
110. Craig D. Feiser, "Protecting the Public's Right to Know: The Debate Over Privatization and Access to Government Information Under State Law," *Florida State University Law Review* 27 (2000): 825–64.
111. Jonathan Turley, "Presidential Papers and Popular Government: The Convergence of Constitutional and Property Theory in Claims of Ownership and Control of Presidential Records," *Cornell Law Review* 88 (2003): 651.
112. Turley, "Presidential Papers," 659–60.

113. On June 30, 1941, at the dedication of the library he established, Franklin Roosevelt said: "To bring together the records of the past and to house them in buildings where they will be preserved for the use of men and women in the future, a Nation must believe in three things.... It must, above all, believe in the capacity of its own people so to learn from the past that they can gain in judgment in creating their own future." "Remarks at the Dedication of the Franklin D. Roosevelt Library at Hyde Park, New York, 1941," in *The Public Papers and Addresses of Franklin Delano Roosevelt* comp. Samuel I. Rosenman (New York: Russell & Russell, 1969), 241.
114. The Presidential Library System was established by Congress in 1955. Act of Aug. 12, 1955, ch. 859, 69 Stat. 695 (codified as amended at 44 U.S.C. 2101, 2107–2108 [2006]).
115. Turley, "Presidential Papers," 666–71.
116. Article 6, "Right to Receive Information from State and Municipal Institutions and Agencies," Law on Provision of Information to the Public (2004).
117. Article 14(3), Law on Provision of Information to the Public (2004).
118. Charles L. Allen, *A Series of Articles on Public Notice* (Stillwater, OK: Oklahoma Press Association, 1964), 7–8.
119. Shannon E. Martin, witness in Bosnia-Herzegovina countryside government notices posted on trees, lampposts, and fountains, 2000.
120. Lauren A. Rieders, "Old Principles, New Technology and the Future of Notice in Newspapers," *Hofstra Law Review* 38, no. 3 (2010): 1009–1043.
121. See, for example, *Clement v. Graham*, 78 Vt. 290, 315, 63 Atlantic Reporter 146, (1906).
122. John Rayner, *A Digest of the Law Concerning Libels: Containing the Resolutions in the Books on the Subject, and Many Manuscript Cases* (London, 1770), p. v. Book owned and annotated by Samuel Chase, housed in the Clements Library, University of Michigan.
123. *An Appeal to the Public in Behalf of George Johnstone, Governor of West-Florida, in Answer to the North Briton Extraordinary, and in Consequence of Other Matters Not Taken Notice of in That Extraordinary Publication* (London: Printed for C Moran, 1763).
124. *Herbert v. Ashburner*, 95 Eng. Rep. 628, Hilary Term, 24 Geo. II 297 (1750).
125. U.S. Statutes at Large, Vol. 1, 1st Congress, 1st Session, Chapter 14 (September 15, 1789).
126. James Boyle, *Shamans, Software and Spleens: Law and the Construction of the Information Society* (Cambridge, MA: Harvard University Press, 1996).
127. Gilbert Bailey, *Legal Advertising* (Bloomington: Indiana University Bureau of Government Research, 1941), 28–29.
128. Shannon E. Martin, "State Laws Mandating Online Posting of Legal and Public Notices Traditionally Published in Newspapers," *Communications and the Law* 25, no. 1 (April 2003): 41–54.
129. Shannon E. Martin, "State-Level Legislative and Court Activity 2006–2007," http://watchnotice.wordpress.com/research/2007–2/, viewed February 2013.
130. Shannon E. Martin, "Snapshot Summary Data for Public Notice Laws in Each State of the U.S.," http://watchnotice.wordpress.com/research/2011–2/, viewed February 2013.
131. Bailey, *Legal Advertising*, iv.
132. Henry Sumner Maine, *Maine's Ancient Law* (New York: Dorset Press, 1861; repr. 1986), 12–15.

133. *Leges Duodecim Tabularum*, or *Duodecim Tabulae*, established basic procedural rights for all Roman citizens against one another. They were presented on two ivory tablets and posted in the Roman Forum so that everyone could read them.
134. James Bryce, *Studies in History and Jurisprudence* (New York: Oxford University Press, 1901), 751–61.
135. Bryce, *Studies in History and Jurisprudence*, 275–76.
136. C.H. McIlwain, *Constitutionalism and the Changing World* (New York: Macmillan, 1939), 127–28.
137. William Blackstone, *Blackstone's Commentaries on the Laws of England* (London: Cavendish Publishing, 2001), Book I, Ch. II, 185.
138. McIlwain, *Constitutionalism and the Changing World*, 168; Bailey, *Legal Advertising*, 4–5.
139. McIlwain, *Constitutionalism and the Changing World*, 169.
140. Preetu Nair, "UGC Issues Public Notice on Lecturer/Assistant Professor Qualifications," *Times of India*, December 21, 2012; Richi Erma, "DDA to Complete Master Plan Review by mid-2013," *Times of India*, February 3, 2013; "Mother Disowns Mafatlal Scion as Her Legal Heir," *Times of India*, October 12, 2012.
141. *Black's Law Dictionary*, 6th ed. (St. Paul, MN: West Publishing, 1990).
142. Shannon E. Martin and Kathleen A. Hansen, "Examining the 'Virtual' Publication as a 'Newspaper of Record,'" *Communication Law and Policy* 1, no. 4 (1996): 579–94; Shannon E. Martin, "State Laws Mandating Online Posting of Legal and Public Notices Traditionally Published in Newspapers," *Communications and the Law* 25, no. 1 (April 2003), 41–54.
143. William Pratt Wade, *A Treatise on the Law of Notice as Affecting Civil Rights and Remedies*, 2nd ed. (Chicago: Calligahan and Co., 1886), 538.
144. Wade, *Treatise*, 539.
145. Wade, *Treatise*, 550.
146. Wade, *Treatise*, 554.
147. See Maurice H. Merrill, "The Anatomy of Notice," *University of Chicago Law Review* 3 (1936): 417.
148. Maurice H. Merrill, *Merrill on Notice: A Comprehensive Treatise on the Principles and Practice of Legal Notice* (Kansas City, MO: Vernon Law Book Co., 1952), 80.
149. Merrill, *Merrill on Notice*, 2.
150. Merrill, *Merrill on Notice*, 3.
151. 35 U.S.C.S. §209, Patentability of Inventions and Grant of Patents, Chapter 18. Patent Rights in Inventions made with Federal Assistance (2013).
152. 47 U.S.C.S. §254, Telegraphs, Telephone, and Radiotelegraphs, Chapter 5. Wire or Radio Communication Common Carriers Development of Competitive Markets ELEGR (2013).
153. 33 U.S.C.S. §1319 Navigation and Navigable Waters, Chapter 26. Water Pollution Prevention and Control Standards and Enforcement (2013).
154. 49 U.S.C.S. §30119, Transportation, Subtitle VI. Motor Vehicle and Driver Programs, Part A, General Chapter 301 Motor Vehicle Safety Subchapter II, Standards and Compliance (2013).
155. Acts and Regulations Publication Act 1989, No. 142, Sections 18–35 (2007), http://www.legislation.govt.nz/act/public/1989/0142/latest/DLM195098.html, viewed March 2013.

156. Fact Sheet No. 1, The Legislative Process in Tanzania, Publication of Bills, http://www.parliament.go.tz/index.php/home/pages/15, viewed March 2013.
157. The Local Electoral Act of 2001, New Zealand, http://www.legislation.govt.nz/act/public/2001/0035/latest/DLM94309.html, viewed March 2013.
158. The Electoral Amendment Act 2002, New Zealand, http://www.legislation.govt.nz/act/public/2002/0001/latest/DLM130605.html, viewed March 2013.
159. The Constitution of the Independent State of Samoa, as amended 2005, Election of the Head of State, First Schedule, Article 18.
160. The Political Constitution of the United Mexican States, as Amended to 2010, States of the Federation and the Federal District, Fifth Title, Article 115.
161. Constitution of Kenya, 2010. See, for example, sections 144, 148, 154, 155, 158, 167, 190, and Article 262, Transitional and Consequential Provisions, Commission for the Implementation of the Constitution.
162. The Procurement Act of 2004, Sierra Leone, No. 14, Part IV, General Provisions on Procurement Proceedings, Section 26, Public Notice of Contract Awards.
163. Biological Diversity Act of 2002, No. 18 of 2003, February 5, 2003.
164. Bankruptcy Act of 2004, Act No. 75, June 2, 2004, amended in 2006 by Act No. 109.
165. Japan Bankruptcy Act of 2004, Article 26.
166. Japan Bankruptcy Act of 2004, Article 32.
167. Japan Bankruptcy Act of 2004, Article 136.
168. Japan Bankruptcy Act of 2004, Article 139.
169. Japan Bankruptcy Act of 2004, Article 197.
170. Japan Bankruptcy Act of 2004, Chapter IX, Article 216.
171. Treaty Between the United States and Senegal Concerning the Reciprocal Encourage and Protection of Investment, Article III, 1(e), 1983.
172. Treaty of Friendship, Commerce and Navigation between the U.S. and the Republic of Korea, Article XIV 3(a), 1956.
173. *Herbert v. Ashburner*, 95 Eng. Rep. 628, Hilary Term, 24 Geo. II 297 (1750).
174. *Rex v. The Guardians, et al.*, 109 Eng. Rep. 202, 9 B. & C. 541, 542 (1829).
175. Shannon E. Martin and David Copeland, eds., *The Function of Newspapers in Society: A Global Perspective* (Westport, CT: Greenwood Publishing, 2003).
176. David A. Copeland, *Colonial American Newspapers: Character and Content* (Newark: University of Delaware Press, 1997); David A. Copeland, *Debating the Issues in Colonial Newspapers: Primary Documents on Events of the Period* (Westport, CT: Greenwood Publishing, 2000).
177. Roger Sherman, "A Citizen of New Haven," No. 15, Thursday, December 25, 1788, in *Essays on the Constitution of the United States*, ed. Paul Leicester Ford (Brooklyn, NY: Historical Printing Club, 1892), 239.
178. Shannon E. Martin and Kathleen A. Hansen, "The Legal System and 'Legal Notices' in Newspapers," in *Newspapers of Record in a Digital Age: From Hot Type to Hot Link* (Westport, CT: Praeger, 1998).
179. In order to assure reasonably current references, the websites noted in this chapter were reviewed as close to the publication date as possible. The "viewed" date included here indicates the most recent access of each particular URL.

180. Site visited: http://panynj.gov/airports/, viewed April 2013. Letter from Susan M. Baer, director, Aviation Department of the Port Authority of New York and New Jersey.
181. A. Jay Wagner and Shannon E. Martin, "Tell It to Me Straight: Opinion on Public Notice," conference paper, MAPOR, 2013.
182. David Cuillier and Suzanne J. Piotrowski, "Internet Information-Seeking and Its Relation to Support for Access to Government Records," *Government Information Quarterly* 26, no. 3 (2009): 441–49; Marc Holzer and Aroon Manoharan, *Digital Governance in Municipalities Worldwide (2011–12): Fifth Global E-Governance Survey: A Longitudinal Assessment of Municipal Websites Throughout the World* (Newark, NJ: Rutgers University E-Governance Institute, National Center for Public Performance, 2012).
183. Daekyung Kim and Thomas J. Johnson, "A Shift in Media Credibility: Comparing Internet and Traditional News," *International Communication Gazette* 71, no. 4 (June 2009): 283–302; Thomas J. Johnson and Barbara K. Kaye, "Cruising Is Believing? Comparing Internet and Traditional Sources on Media Credibility Measures," *Journalism and Mass Communication Quarterly* 75, no. 2 (June 1998): 325–40; Thomas J. Johnson and Barbara K. Kaye, "Using Is Believing: The Influence of Reliance on the Credibility of Online Political Information Among Politically Interested Internet Users," *Journalism and Mass Communication Quarterly* 77, no 4 (Winter 2000): 865–79; Thomas J. Johnson and Barbara K. Kaye, "Still Cruising and Believing? An Analysis of Online Credibility Across Three Presidential Campaigns," *American Behavioral Scientist* 54, no. 1 (September 2010): 57–77; M. Jae Moon, "The Evolution of E-Government among Municipalities: Rhetoric or Reality?" *Public Administration Review* 62, no 4. (July/August 2002): 424–33; Suzanne J. Piotrowski and E.L. Borry, "Governmental Transparency and Websites: The Case of New Jersey Municipalities," in *Strategies for Local E-Government Adoption and Implementation: Comparative Studies*, ed. C.G. Reddick (Hershey, PA: IGI Global, 2009); Suzanne J. Piotrowski and Gregg G. Van Ryzin, "Citizen Attitudes Toward Transparency in Local Government," *American Review of Public Administration* 37, no. 3 (September 2007): 306–23.
184. Data collected May 3–May 10, 2012. The respondents: 52 male, 78 white, average age 39.8. The survey instrument: 64 questions, estimated completion time 15 minutes. The survey was generally about information source selection and development of public opinion. Questions for this study focused on a set of questions directly concerning opinion on public notification.
185. http://thepublicnotice.org/about/, viewed May 28, 2013.
186. http://thepublicnotice.org/about/staff/, viewed May 28, 2013.
187. http://thepublicnotice.org/terms-of-use/, viewed May 28, 2013.
188. http://thepublicnotice.org/about/faq/, viewed May 28, 2013.
189. http://www.noticeandcomment.com/how-to-use-this-site.aspx, viewed June 4, 2013.
190. http://www.noticeandcomment.com/about-us.aspx, viewed June 4, 2013.
191. http://www.noticeandcomment.com/search-press-releases.aspx, viewed June 4, 2013.
192. The form of government for individual country will be noted as listed on the World Factbook, https://www.cia.gov/library/publications/the-world-factbook/fields/2128.html, viewed June 3, 2013.
193. Brian A. Curran and others, *Obelisk: A History* (Cambridge, MA: MIT Press, 2009).

194. For the purposes of this chapter, an Internet user is one who has access to an Internet connection and has the basic knowledge required to use web technology. The starting age of those included as users varied from country to country. This definition is taken from the Internet World Stats Website, "Surfing and Site Guide," About Us, http://www.internetworldstats.com/surfing.htm, viewed June 12, 2013.
195. "Internet users, Population and Facebook Statistics for Africa, 2012," Internet World Stats, www.internetworldstats.com, viewed May 31, 2013.
196. See http://www.ictregulationtoolkit.org/en/Publication.3573.html, viewed June 4, 2013.
197. http://www.arpt.dz/fr/pub/bult/, viewed June 4, 2013.
198. http://www.algerianembassy.org/consular_affairs/moving.html, viewed June 4, 2013.
199. http://www.nairaland.com/64903/central-bank-nigeria-public-notice, viewed June 4, 2013.
200. http://www.copyright.gov.ng/index.php/public-notice, viewed June 4, 2013.
201. http://www.nercng.org/index.php/media-and-publicity/public-notices, viewed June 4, 2013.
202. http://www.iam.ma/Lists/Tlchargement20Finance/Attachments/345/MarocTelecom-Document-Reference-2010-VERSION-ANGLAISE.pdf, viewed June 4, 2013.
203. "Internet users, population and Facebook statistics for Africa, 2012."
204. http://www.emergence.gov.ma/en/Pacte/Pages/LePacte.aspx, viewed June 5, 2013.
205. http://www.anp.org.ma/En/Agency/Pages/Governance.aspx, viewed June 5, 2013.
206. http://adala.justice.gov.ma/production/Guides_Manuels/fr/PlaquetteANG.pdf, viewed June 5, 2013.
207. http://www.service-public.ma/en/Web/guest/, viewed June 5, 2013.
208. "Egypt: Cairo's Tahrir Square Fills with Protesters," BBC, July 8, 2011, archived from the original on July 9, 2011, viewed June 5, 2013.
209. http://www.washington.edu/news/2011/09/12/new-study-quantifies-use-of-social-media-in-arab-spring/, viewed June 5, 2013.
210. http://www.eip.gov.eg/AboutEIP/AboutEIP.aspx, viewed June 5, 2013.
211. http://www.idsc.gov.eg/default.aspx, viewed June 5, 2013.
212. "Internet Users in the Middle East, June 30, 2012," www.internetworldstats.com, viewed June 5, 2013.
213. For example, http://dosfan.lib.uic.edu/ERC/cpa/english/regulations/PN1.pdf, viewed June 5, 2013.
214. http://www.dod.mil/pubs/foi/operation_and_plans/CPA_ORHA/11_F_0117Doc94_Coalition_Provisional_Authority_Public_Notice_Regarding_Creation_of_Iraqi_Central_Bank_DevelopmentFund_forIraq.pdf, viewed June 5, 2013.
215. For example, the "Public Notice for VSAT Operators" at http://www.cmc.iq/en/pdfcmc/CMC VSAT public notice.pdf, viewed June 5, 2013; "Investor Guide," at http://www.mofa.gov.iq/documentfiles/InvestorGuide.pdf, viewed June 5, 2013.
216. http://www.isc.gov.iq/sites/isc.gov.iq/files/SecuritiesLawEnglishversion.pdf, p. 27, viewed June 5, 2013.
217. http://www.health.gov.il/English/Services/MedicalAndHealthProfessions/Occpational-Therapist/Pages/Notice.aspx, viewed June 5, 2013.
218. http://www.iaa.gov.il/Rashat/en-US/Rashot/MessagesArchive/SpokesMan/msg151012.htm, viewed June 5, 2013.

219. http://www.netanya.muni.il/Eng/?CategoryID=1598&ArticleID=2144, viewed June 5, 2013.
220. "Internet Users, Population and Facebook Statistics for the Middle East, 2012," Internet World Stats, www.internetworldstats.com, viewed June 12, 2013.
221. http://www.lgchem.com.tr/products/16122012–181558-msds_lg411_e.pdf, viewed June 12, 2013.
222. http://www.mfa.gov.tr/chapter-i_-conditions-of-residence-and-business.en.mfa, viewed June 12, 2013.
223. http://akademi.tuba.gov.tr/en/haberler/tuba-dan-haberler/kurumdan-haberler/1580-tuerkye-blmler-akadems-kamuoyu-bldrs.html, viewed June 12, 2013.
224. http://www.nesibeaydin.k12.tr/okul/index.php?option=com_content&view=article&id=447:emniyet-genel-mueduerluegue-kamu-spotu&catid=94&Itemid=511&lang=en, viewed June 12, 2013.
225. http://en.service-public-particuliers.gouv.mc/, viewed June 12, 2013.
226. http://en.service-public-entreprises.gouv.mc/, viewed June 12, 2013.
227. http://en.service-public-particuliers.gouv.mc/You-and-The-Administration/Honours/Honours/How-to-nominate-someone-for-an-honorary-distinction, viewed June 12, 2013.
228. http://en.service-public-particuliers.gouv.mc/Announcements2/Stamps-to-go-on-sale-on-5-July-2013, viewed June 12, 2013.
229. http://en.service-public-particuliers.gouv.mc/Announcements2/List-of-paid-public-holidays-in-2013, viewed June 12, 2013.
230. http://www.wambrechies.fr/Services-en-ligne/Actualites/Avis-public, viewed June 12, 2013.
231. http://www.pays-de-lure.fr/vivre_en_pays_de_lure/avis-public-insertion-1.pdf, viewed June 12, 2013.
232. http://www.ville-avion.fr/-Avis-public-.html, viewed June 12, 2013.
233. http://www.nice.fr/Media/Files/Avis-public-POS, viewed June 12, 2013.
234. http://www.finanznachrichten.de/nachrichten-2013–04/26489102-public-notice-on-potentially-hazardous-appliance-wiring-008.htm, viewed June 12, 2013.
235. http://www.metrogroup.de/internet/site/metrogroup/get/documents/metrogroup_international/corpsite/05_inrel/publications/disclosures-13–01–04-ASKO-en.pdf, viewed June 12, 2013.
236. http://www.google.com/url?sa=t&rct=j&q=&esrc=s&source=Web&cd=19&ved=0CFgQFjAIOAo&url=http 3A 2F 2Fwww.vilp.de 2FpdfGeneration 3Fid 3D1289 26lang 3Dpl&ei=FsS4Uen7K6nm0gHlwYDoBA&usg=AFQjCNHkRwMvQytZqeUNFssPtpCs1HhMuQ&bvm=bv.47810305,d.dmQ, viewed June 12, 2013.
237. http://australia.gov.au/news-and-media/public-consultations, viewed June 13, 2013.
238. http://australia.gov.au/publications/australian-government-gazettes#GovernmentNoticesGazette, viewed June 13, 2013.
239. http://www.dia.govt.nz/Services-New-Zealand-Gazette-Index, viewed June 13, 2013.
240. http://www.bankpng.gov.pg/exchange-control-mainmenu-138/public-notice, viewed June 13, 2013.
241. http://www.lands.gov.pg/Public_Notice/Secretary.html, viewed June 13, 2013.

242. http://mail.pangtel.gov.pg/Pages/Home.aspx, viewed June 13, 2013.
243. http://www.pngports.com.pg/docs/Public-notices/PNGPCL_CCD1011_PUBLIC-NOTICE-Queens-Birthday.pdf, viewed June 13, 2013.
244. See, for example, http://www.mtsl.com.pg/main/href/0c/news/; http://www.unitech.ac.pg/index.php?option=com_content&view=article&id=74:public-notice&catid=169:news-public-notices&Itemid=89; http://www.postcourier.com.pg/20120502/news01.htm, all viewed June 12, 2013.
245. For example, http://www.doe.gov.bz/documents/EIA/Chrysalis/Annex 20X – Public_Consultation_Report_for_Chrysalis Edited.pdf; http://www.doe.gov.bz/ECP/ECPs/Belize ECPs/BZE 2004 ECPs/Belize Fifth Power Development Project 2004 ECPL.pdf; http://www.doe.gov.bz/, all viewed June 13, 2013.
246. http://www.elections.gov.bz/modules/article_publish/files/files_4918ec65aafb8.pdf, p. 152, viewed June 13, 2013.
247. http://www.puntofocal.gov.ar/doc/2a104belice.pdf, viewed June 13, 2013.
248. http://www.scp.com.ar/doc/SituacionConcursal/SCP-Edicto_Asamblea_22–06–12.pdf, viewed June 19, 2013.
249. http://www.frioindustrias.com.ar/actual/en/new.htm, viewed June 19, 2013.
250. http://www.puntofocal.gov.ar/notific_otros_miembros/tpkm34_t.pdf, viewed June 19, 2013.
251. http://www.itamaraty.gov.br/temas/difusao-cultural/iv-concurso-internacional-de-monografias-lygia-fagundes-telles/iv-concurso-internacional-de-monografias-lygia-fagundes-telles-ing, viewed June 19, 2013.
252. http://www.brasil.gov.br/news/history/2012/11/12/mercosur-launches-public-notice-in-december-to-award-projects-to-eradicate-poverty-and-combat-hunger/newsitem_view?set_language=en, viewed June 19, 2013.
253. http://www.museuartesacra.org.br/WYRPublicNotice.pdf, viewed June 19, 2013.
254. http://www.indecopi.gob.pe/repositorioaps/0/5/jer/legislation_ve/Trade_Remedies_US.pdf, viewed June 19, 2013.
255. http://www.sgs.pe/en/Logistics/Transportation/Containers/Pre-Shipment-Inspection-PSI/Pre-Shipment-Inspection-Angola.aspx, viewed June 19, 2013.
256. http://www.puertodeguaymas.com.mx/news/46-home/193-the-port-of-guaymas-public-notice-to-those-interested-in-participating-in-the-process-of-opening-to-private-investment, viewed June 19, 2013.
257. http://pooplus.x10.mx/forms/FL-DWC-250-i.pdf, viewed June 19, 2013.
258. http://dof.gob.mx/copias.php?acc=ajaxPaginas&paginas=78&seccion=PRIMERA&edicion=218369&ed=MATUTINO&fecha=25/02/2009, viewed June 19, 2013.
259. See, for example, http://articles.timesofindia.indiatimes.com/2013–06–09/goa/39849159_1_shacks-tourism-department-tourism-season, viewed June 19, 2013.
260. http://www.ilntoday.com/files/2012/08/ZL-Newsletter_201208.pdf, viewed June 24, 2013.
261. See, for example, http://www.prnewswire.com/news-releases/public-notice-on-potentially-hazardous-appliance-wiring-202314351.html, viewed June 24, 2013.
262. See, for example, http://newspapers.nl.sg/Digitised/Article/straitstimes19160524–1.2.47.aspx, viewed June 24, 2013.

263. http://www.apeccp.org.tw/doc/Taipei/Decision/ctdec037.htm; http://english.taipei.gov.tw/ct.asp?xItem=1803812&ctNode=32871&mp=100002; http://www.itri.org.tw/eng/econtent/copyright/copyright01.aspx, all viewed June 24, 2013.
264. See, for example, an unpublished opinion of the California Court of Appeals, Lexis 3983, 38 Media L. Rep. 1975 (2010), 43 Conn. App. 563, 684 A.2d 1207 (1996), 835 N.E.2d 235 (2005) from Indiana.
265. Idaho 60–106A (2011).
266. Kentucky 38 KRS 424.195 (2010).
267. Nebraska 33–141–142 (2010).
268. Missouri 9.115.127 (2011).
269. New Jersey 40A:11–5(1)(j) (2011).
270. http://www.acfcs.org/federal-forfeiture-notices-will-soon-be-on-line-only/, http://www.boston.com/news/politics/politicalintelligence/2009/04/obama_to_cabine.html, http://voices.washingtonpost.com/federal-eye/2009/04/trimming_the_federal_fat_part.html, all viewed July 22, 2013.
271. Site viewed July 16, 2013.
272. http://www.mypublicnotices.com/PublicNotice.asp?Page=WhatArePublicNotices, viewed July 16, 2013.
273. http://www.dia.govt.nz/diawebsite.nsf/wpg_URL/Services-New-Zealand-Gazette-Legal-Policies?OpenDocument, viewed July 18, 2013.
274. http://www.dia.govt.nz/Data-and-statistics, viewed July 18, 2013.
275. https://data.govt.nz/latest-data-requests/, viewed July 18, 2013.
276. See, for example, Shannon E. Martin, *Freedom of Information: The News the Media Use* (New York: Peter Lang, 2008).
277. See, for example, domestic websites dedicated to public notice of a certain type, such as http://www.law.com/jsp/pa/specials.jsp?p=public_notices, sponsored by the Legal Intelligencer, or the previously noted http://thepublicnotice.org/ sponsored by private donations, viewed July 17, 2013.
278. http://i-uv.com/post-your-courtesy-notices-for-the-world-community-to-acknowledge/, viewed July 17, 2013.
279. http://www.globaltenders.com/index.htm, viewed July 17, 2013. The list of countries includes Afghanistan, Albania, Algeria, American Samoa, Argentina, Armenia, Australia, Austria, Azerbaijan, Bahrain, Bangladesh, Barbados, Belarus, Belgium, Belize, Benin, Bhutan, Bolivia, Bosnia and Herzegovina, Botswana, Brazil, Brunei Darussalam, Bulgaria, Burkina Faso, Burundi, Cambodia, Cameroon, Canada, Chad, Chile, China, Colombia, Costa Rica, Cote d'Ivoire, Croatia, Cuba, Cyprus, Czech Republic, Denmark, Ecuador, Egypt, El Salvador, Estonia, Ethiopia, Finland, France, Gambia, Georgia, Germany, Ghana, Greece, Guatemala, Guyana, Haiti, Honduras, Hong Kong, Hungary, Iceland, India, Indonesia, Iran (Islamic Republic of), Iraq, Ireland, Israel, Italy, Jamaica, Japan, Jordan, Kazakhstan, Kenya, Kiribati, Korea (Democratic People's Republic of), Korea (Republic of), Kuwait, Kyrgyzstan, Lao People's Democratic Republic, Latvia, Lebanon, Lesotho, Liberia, Libyan Arab Jamahiriya, Liechtenstein, Lithuania, Luxembourg, Macau, Macedonia (Republic of), Madagascar, Malawi, Malaysia, Maldives, Mali, Malta, Mauritius, Mexico, Micronesia (Federated States of), Moldova (Republic of), Monaco, Mongolia, Montser-

rat, Morocco, Mozambique, Myanmar, Namibia, Nepal, Netherlands, New Zealand, Nicaragua, Niger, Nigeria, Norway, Oman, Pakistan, Panama, Paraguay, Peru, Philippines, Poland, Portugal, Puerto Rico, Qatar, Romania, Russian Federation, Rwanda, Saudi Arabia, Senegal, Serbia, Serbia and Montenegro, Seychelles, Sierra Leone, Singapore, Slovakia, Slovenia, South Africa, Spain, Sri Lanka, Sudan, Sweden, Switzerland, Syrian Arab Republic, Taiwan (Province of) China, Tajikistan, Tanzania (United Republic of), Thailand, Tunisia, Turkey, Turkmenistan, Uganda, Ukraine, United Arab Emirates, United Kingdom, United States, Uruguay, Uzbekistan, Venezuela, Viet Nam, Yemen, Yugoslavia, Zambia, and Zimbabwe.

280. http://www.globaltenders.com/global_tenders_FAQ.htm, viewed July 17, 2013.
281. http://courtsad.blogspot.com/p/blog-page.html, viewed July 17, 2013.
282. See, for example, the specifics of business public notices: http://en.service-public-entreprises.gouv.mc/Tax/VAT/Statements/Invoices-Obligatory-notices, viewed July 17, 2013; and http://en.service-public-entreprises.gouv.mc/Tax/VAT/Statements/Invoices-Obligatory-notices, viewed July 22, 2013.
283. http://www.archives.gov.il/ArchiveGov_Eng/about/Notices2/, viewed July 22, 2013.
284. http://www.archives.gov.il/ArchiveGov_Eng/Our+Holdings/collection/, viewed July 22, 2013.
285. http://dgm.export.gov.il/, viewed July 22, 2013.
286. "Guidelines for Digital Newspaper Preservation Readiness," 3, http://publishing.educopia.org/chronicles/, viewed July 23, 2013.
287. There are many estimates available. For example, see "Public Policy and Funding the News: Insult to Injury," http://fundingthenews.usc.edu/related_research/6_Carnegie_PublicNotice.pdf, viewed July 22, 2013; "Move to Online Public Notices Looms over Newspapers," http://usatoday30.usatoday.com/tech/news/2009–05–22-online-notices_N.htm, viewed July 22, 2013.
288. http://www.acfcs.org/federal-forfeiture-notices-will-soon-be-on-line-only/; http://www.boston.com/news/politics/politicalintelligence/2009/04/obama_to_cabine.html; http://voices.washingtonpost.com/federal-eye/2009/04/trimming_the_federal_fat_part.html, all viewed July 22, 2013.
289. http://www.forfeiture.gov/, viewed July 22, 2013.
290. http://www.bid4assets.com/storefront/index.cfm?fuseaction=govtassets&sfid=21, viewed July 22, 2013.
291. See, for example, Vannevar Bush, "As We May Think," *The Atlantic*, July 1, 1945, http://www.theatlantic.com/magazine/archive/1945/07/as-we-may-think/303881/, viewed July 29, 2013; Ernst Posner, *American State Archives* (Chicago: University of Chicago Press, 1964); H.G. Jones, *Local Government Records: An Introduction to Their Management, Preservation, and Use* (Nashville, TN: American Association for State and Local History), 1980.
292. See, for example, Suzanna Conrad, "Key Issues," *Prairienet*, http://www.prairienet.org/op/digarch/key-issues/; Margaret Hedstrom, "Digital Preservation: Problems and Prospects," http://www.dl.slis.tsukuba.ac.jp/DLjournal/No_20/1-hedstrom/1-hedstrom.html; "History Flushed, *The Economist*, April 28, 2012, http://www.economist.com/node/21553410; all viewed July 29, 2013.

293. Catharine Giordano, archives assistant/editorial researcher, *Stars and Stripes*, July 29, 2013, newslib listserv.
294. Linda Deitch, archive and collections manager, The Columbus Dispatch Library, Columbus, Ohio, July 29, 2013, newslib listserv.
295. See, for example, data security policy issues at the turn of the century, http://www.sans.org/reading_room/whitepapers/backup/electronic-data-retention-policy_514, viewed July 29, 2013.
296. Peter Steiner, *The New Yorker*, July 5, 1993, p. 61.
297. *Kevin Fisher et al. v. Rutherford County Regional Planning Commission et al.*, No. M2012–01397-COA–R3–CV, Court of Appeals of Tennessee (Nashville), May 29, 2013.

LIST OF FIGURES

BIBLIOGRAPHY OF PRINTED WORKS

Adams, John. *History of the Dispute with America from Its Origin in 1754*. London: J. Stockdale, 1784.

Allen, Charles L. *A Series of Articles on Public Notice*. Stillwater, OK: Oklahoma Press Association, 1964.

Avrin, Leila. *Scribes, Script, and Books: The Book Arts from Antiquity to the Renaissance*. Chicago: American Library Association, 1991.

Backes, Ronald. "Freedom, Information, Security." *Seton Hall Constitutional Law Journal* 10 (Summer 2000): 927–1003.

Bailey, Gilbert. *Legal Advertising*. Bloomington: Indiana University Bureau of Government Research, 1941.

Black's Law Dictionary. 6th ed. St. Paul, MN: West Publishing, 1990.

Blackstone, William. *Blackstone's Commentaries on the Laws of England*. London: Cavendish Publishing, 2001. See esp. vol. I, chap. 7, "Of the Parliament."

Bluhm, William Theodore. *Theories of the Political System: Classics of Political Thought and Modern Political Analysis*. 3rd ed. London: Prentice-Hall, 1978.

Boyce, George, James Curran, and Pauline Wingate, eds. *Newspaper History from the 17th Century to the Present Day*. Beverly Hills, CA: Sage Publications, 1978.

Boyle, James. *Shamans, Software and Spleens: Law and the Construction of the Information Society*. Cambridge, MA: Harvard University Press, 1996.

Brown, Richard D. *Knowledge Is Power: The Diffusion of Information in Early America, 1700–1865*. New York: Oxford University Press, 1989.

Bryce, James. *Studies in History and Jurisprudence*. New York: Oxford University Press, 1901.

Casson, Lionel. *Libraries in the Ancient World.* New Haven, CT: Yale University Press, 2001.

Clark, Charles E. *The Public Prints: The Newspaper in Anglo-American Culture.* New York: Oxford University Press, 1994.

Cole, John Y. *Jefferson's Legacy: A Brief History of the Library of Congress.* Washington, DC: Library of Congress, 1993.

Copeland, David A. *Colonial American Newspapers: Character and Content.* Newark: University of Delaware Press, 1997.

Copeland, David A. *Debating the Issues in Colonial Newspapers: Primary Documents on Events of the Period.* Westport, CT: Greenwood Press, 2000.

Cross, Harold L. *The People's Right to Know: Legal Access to Public Records and Proceedings.* New York: Columbia University Press, 1953.

Cuillier, David, and Suzanne J. Piotrowski. "Internet Information-Seeking and Its Relation to Support for Access to Government Records." *Government Information Quarterly* 26, no. 3 (July 2009): 441–49.

Curran, Brian A., Anthony Grafton, Pamela O. Long, and Benjamin Weiss. *Obelisk: A History.* Cambridge, MA: MIT Press, 2009.

Driscoll, P.D., S.L. Splichal, M.B. Salwen, and B. Garrison. "Public Support for Access to Government Records: A National Survey." In *Access Denied: Freedom of Information in the Information Age*, edited by C.N. Davis and S.L. Splichal, 23–36. Ames: Iowa State University Press, 2000.

Eisenstein, Elizabeth. *The Printing Press as an Agent of Change: Communications and Cultural Transformations in Early Modern Europe.* Cambridge: Cambridge University Press, 1979.

Erma, Richi. "DDA to Complete Master Plan Review by Mid-2013." *Times of India*, February 3, 2013.

Feiser, Craig D. "Protecting the Public's Right to Know: The Debate Over Privatization and Access to Government Information Under State Law." *Florida State University Law Review* 27 (2000): 825–64.

Foerstel, Herbert N. *Freedom of Information and the Right to Know: Origins and Applications of the Freedom of Information Act.* Westport, CT: Greenwood Press, 1999.

Ford, Paul Leicester, ed. *Essays on the Constitution of the United States*. Brooklyn, NY: Historical Printing Club, 1892.

Ford, Paul Leicester, ed. *Pamphlets on the Constitution of the United States: Published During Its Discussion by the People, 1787–1788.* Brooklyn, NY: n.p., 1888.

Ford, Paul Leicester, ed. *The Writings of Thomas Jefferson.* 12 vols. New York: Putnam, 1904.

Frank, Joseph. *The Beginnings of the English Newspaper: 1620–1660.* Cambridge, MA: Harvard University Press, 1961.

Gellhorn, Walter. "The Administrative Procedures Act: The Beginnings." *Virginia Law Review* 72, no. 2 (March 1986): 219–33.

Grabler, Susan Lee. "Government Information of, by, and for the People: The Changing Mission of the American Library Association's Public Documents Committee, 1876–1956." *Journal of Government Information* 22, no. 1 (1995): 45–69.

Hoefges, Michael, Martin E. Halstuk, and Bill F. Chamberlin. "Privacy Rights Versus FOIA Disclosure Policy: The 'Uses and Effects' Double Standard in Access to Personally-Identifiable

Information in Government Records." *William & Mary Bill of Rights Journal* 12, no. 1 (2003): 1.

Holmes, David. *Communication Theory: Media, Technology and Society*. Thousand Oaks, CA: Sage, 2005.

Johnson, Thomas J., and Barbara K. Kaye. "Cruising Is Believing? Comparing Internet and Traditional Sources on Media Credibility Measures." *Journalism and Mass Communication Quarterly* 75, no. 2 (June 1998): 325–40.

Johnson, Thomas J., and Barbara K. Kaye. "Still Cruising and Believing? An Analysis of Online Credibility Across Three Presidential Campaigns." *American Behavioral Scientist* 54, no. 1 (Sept. 2010): 57–77.

Johnson, Thomas J., and Barbara K. Kaye. "Using Is Believing: The Influence of Reliance on the Credibility of Online Political Information Among Politically Interested Internet Users." *Journalism and Mass Communication Quarterly* 77, no 4. (Winter 2000): 865–79.

Jones, H.G. *Local Government Records: An Introduction to Their Management, Preservation, and Use*. Nashville, TN: American Association for State and Local History, 1980.

Jones, H.G. *The Records of a Nation: Their Management, Preservation, and Use*. New York: Atheneum, 1969.

Kim, Daekyung, and Thomas J. Johnson. "A Shift in Media Credibility: Comparing Internet and Traditional News." *International Communication Gazette* 71, no. 4 (June 2009): 283–302.

Kozinets, Peter S. "Access to the E-Mail Records of Public Officials: Safeguarding the Public's Right to Know." *Communications Lawyer* 25 (Summer 2007): 17.

Kunsch, Kelly. "Diogenes Wanders the Superhighway: A Proposal for Authentication of Publicly Disseminated Documents on the Internet." *Seattle University Law Review* 20 (1997): 49.

Lax, Stephen. "The Internet and Democracy." In *Web Studies: Rewiring Media Studies for the Digital Age*, edited by David Gauntlett. Oxford: Oxford University Press, 2000.

Logan, Wayne A. *Knowledge as Power: Criminal Registration and Community Notification Laws in America*. Stanford, CA: Stanford University Press, 2009.

Madison, James. James Madison to W.T. Barry, 4 August, 1822. In *The Writings of James Madison*, edited by Gaillard Hunt, no. 9. New York: G.P. Putnam's Sons, 1910.

Madison, James, *Notes of Debates in the Federal Convention of 1787 Reported by James Madison*. Introd. by Adrienne Koch. Athens: Ohio University Press, 1985.

Maine, Henry Summer. *Ancient Law: Its Connection with the Early History of Society, and Its Relation to Modern Ideas*. New York: Charles Scribner and Co., 1870.

Martin, Shannon E. *Freedom of Information: The News the Media Use*. New York: Peter Lang, 2008.

Martin, Shannon E. "State Laws Mandating Online Posting of Legal and Public Notices Traditionally Published in Newspapers." *Communications and Law* 25, no. 1 (April 2003): 41–54.

Martin, Shannon E., and David Copeland, eds. *The Function of Newspapers in Society: A Global Perspective*. Westport, CT: Greenwood Publishing, 2003.

Martin, Shannon E., and Kathleen A. Hansen. "Examining the 'Virtual' Publication as a 'Newspaper of Record.'" *Communication Law and Policy* 1, no. 4 (1996): 579–94.

Martin, Shannon E., and Kathleen Hansen. *Newspapers of Record in a Digital Age: From Hot Type to Hot Link.* Westport, CT: Praeger, 1998.

Martin, Shannon E., Bill F. Chamberlin, and Irina Dmitrieva. "State Laws Requiring World Wide Web Dissemination of Information: A Review of State Government Mandates for Documents Online." *Information and Communication Technology Law* 10, no. 2 (June 2001): 169–80.

McIlwain, C.H. *Constitutionalism and the Changing World.* New York: Macmillan, 1939.

McPherson, Elizabeth G. "The Southern States and the Reporting of Senate Debates, 1789–1802." *The Journal of Southern History* 12, no. 2 (May 1946): 223–46.

Merrill, Maurice H. "The Anatomy of Notice." *The University of Chicago Law Review* 3, no. 3 (April 1936): 417–32.

Merrill, Maurice H. *Merrill on Notice: A Comprehensive Treatise on the Principles and Practice of Legal Notice.* Kansas City, MO: Vernon Law Book Co., 1952.

Moon, M. Jae. "The Evolution of E-Government among Municipalities: Rhetoric or Reality?" *Public Administration Review* 62, no 4. (July/August 2002): 424–33.

"Mother Disowns Mafatlal Scion as Her Legal Heir." *Times of India*, October 12, 2012.

Nair, Preetu. "UGC Issues Public Notice on Lecturer/Assistant Professor Qualifications." *Times of India*, December 21, 2012.

Notes of Debates in the Federal Convention of 1787 Reported by James Madison. With an introduction by Adrienne Koch. Athens: Ohio University Press, 1985.

Overholser, Geneva, and Kathleen Hall Jamieson, eds. *The Press.* New York: Oxford University Press, 2005.

Piotrowski, Suzanne J., and E.L. Borry. "Governmental Transparency and Websites: The Case of New Jersey Municipalities." In *Strategies for Local E-Government Adoption and Implementation: Comparative Studies*, edited by C.G. Reddick. Hershey, PA: IGI Global, 2009.

Piotrowski, Suzanne J., and Gregg G. Van Ryzin. "Citizen Attitudes Toward Transparency in Local Government." *The American Review of Public Administration* 37, no. 3 (Sept. 2007): 306–23.

Posner, Ernst. *American State Archives.* Chicago: University of Chicago Press, 1964.

Quinn, Aimee C. "Keeping the Citizenry Informed: Early Congressional Printing and 21st Century Information Policy." *Government Information Quarterly* 20, no. 3 (2003): 281–93.

Read, William Thompson. *Life and Correspondence of George Read.* Philadelphia: J.B. Lippincott & Co., 1870.

Rhodes, P.J. "Public Documents in the Greek States: Archives and Inscriptions." *Greece & Rome* 48, no.1 (April 2001): 33–44.

Rickards, Maurice. *The Public Notice: An Illustrated History.* New York: Crown Publishers, 1973.

Rieders, Lauren A. "Old Principles, New Technology, and the Future of Notice in Newspapers." *Hofstra Law Review* 38, no. 3 (2010): 1009–43.

Rourke, Francis E. "Administrative Secrecy: A Congressional Dilemma." *American Political Science Review* 54, no. 3 (Sept. 1960): 684–94.

Rubin, Edward. "It's Time to Make the Administrative Procedures Act Administrative." *Cornell Law Review* 89 (2003): 93.

Shapiro, Martin. "APA: Past, Present, Future." *Virginia Law Review* 72 (1986): 447–92.

Sherman, Roger. *Remarks on a Pamphlet Entitled, "A Dissertation on the Political Union and Constitution of the Thirteen United States of North America" by "a Citizen of Philadelphia."* Philadelphia: T & B Green, 1784.

Sickinger, James P. *Public Records and Archives in Classical Athens*. Chapel Hill: University of North Carolina Press, 1999.

Turley, Jonathan. "Presidential Papers and Popular Government: The Convergence of Constitutional and Property Theory in Claims of Ownership and Control of Presidential Records." *Cornell Law Review* 88 (2003): 651.

Voltmer, Katrin. "The Media, Government Accountability, and Citizen Engagement." In *Public Sentinel: News Media and Governance Reform*, edited by Pippa Norris. Washington, DC: World Bank, 2010.

Wade, William Pratt. *A Treatise on the Law of Notice as Affecting Civil Rights and Remedies*. 2nd ed. Chicago: Callaghan and Company, 1878.

Wagner, A. Jay, and Shannon E. Martin. "Tell It to Me Straight: Opinion on Public Notice." Paper presented at the Midwest Association for Public Opinion Research (MAPOR) Annual Conference, Chicago, IL, Nov. 2013.

Warren, Samuel D., and Louis D. Brandeis. "The Right to Privacy." *Harvard Law Review* 4, no 5. (Dec. 1890): 193–220.

Wells Branscomb, Anne. *Who Owns Information?* New York: Basic Books, 1994.

Wiggins, James Russell. *Freedom or Secrecy*. New York: Oxford University Press, 1956.

Wolf, Edwin, 2nd. *At the Instance of Benjamin Franklin: A Brief History of the Library Company of Philadelphia, 1731–1976*. Philadelphia, PA: The Library Company of Philadelphia, 1976.

BIBLIOGRAPHY OF WORKS OF LAW

United States of America Constitutions and Statutory Works of Law

Continental Congress, 1774, *Extracts from the votes and proceedings of the American Continental Congress, Held at Philadelphia, on the Fifth of September, 1774*. Published by order of the congress, Philadelphia, Printed (1775). Group 2, pp. 36–37.

U.S. Continental Congress, Resolution 4, *Extracts from the votes and proceedings of the American Continental Congress, Held at Philadelphia, 1774*. Published by order of the congress, Philadelphia, First Group.

U.S. Continental Congress, signed by Henry Middleton, president, *Extracts from the votes and proceedings of the American Continental Congress, Held at Philadelphia, 1774*. Published by order of the congress, Philadelphia, First Group, p. 66–71.

The Declaration of Independence, 1776, lines 109–114.

Articles of Confederation, 1777, lines 45–47, 205–210, 368, 373–384.

U.S. Constitution, Art. II, Sec. 3 (1787).

An Act to provide for the safe-keeping of the Act, Records and Seal of the United States, and for other purposes, First Congress, Session 1, Chapter XIV, September 15, 1789.

United States *Statutes at Large*, Vol. 1, 1st Congress, 1st Session, Chapter 14 (September 15, 1789).

3 *Annals of Congress* 493 (1792).

4 *Annals of Congress* 56 & 250 (1794).

8 *Annals of Congress* 1374–5 (1798).

33 *U.S.C.S.* §1319 Navigation and Navigable Waters, Chapter 26. Water Pollution Prevention and Control Standards and Enforcement (2013).

35 *U.S.C.S.* §209, Patentability of Inventions and Grant of Patents, Chapter 18. Patent Rights in Inventions made with Federal Assistance (2013).

47 *U.S.C.S.* §254, Telegraphs, Telephone, and Radiotelegraphs, Chapter 5. Wire or Radio Communication Common Carriers Development of Competitive Markets ELEGR (2013).

49 *U.S.C.S.* §30119, Transportation, Subtitle VI. Motor Vehicle and Driver Programs, Part A, General Chapter 301 Motor Vehicle Safety Subchapter II, Standards and Compliance (2013).

5 *U.S.C.* 1002, 60 Stat. 238, Administrative Personnel (2013).

Depository Library Act, Pub. L. No. 87–579, 76 Stat. 352 (1962).

Amendment to the Administrative Procedures Act, Pub. L. No. 89–487, 80 Stat. 250 (1966).

Presidential Archival Depository Act of Aug. 12, 1955, ch. 859, 69 *Stat. at Large* 695 (codified as amended at 44 U.S.C. 2101, 2107–2108 [2006]).

Kentucky, Supplementation of printed notice by broadcast in certain cases 38 KRS 424.195 (2010).

Massachusetts Constitution, 1780, art. XVIII.

Memorandum from President Reagan to Heads of Executive Departments and Agencies, Procedures Governing Responses to Congressional Requests for Information, November 4, 1982.

New Jersey Local Government Services, Purchasing 40A:11–5(1)(j) (2011).

Pennsylvania Constitution, 1790, art. I, §14.

United States of America Case Law

Clay v. Ballard, 13 S.E. 262 (Va. 1891).

Clement v. Graham, 78 Vt. 290, 315, 63 Atlantic Reporter 146, (1906).

Cormack v. Wolcott, 15 P. 245 (Kan. 1887).

Ferry v. Williams, 41 N.J.L. 332 (1879).

Marbury v. Madison, 5 U.S. 137 (1803).

Nowack v. Auditor General, 234 Mich. 203–204 (1928).

State v. King, 154 Ind. 625 (1900).

Webber v. Townley, 5 N.W. 971 (Mich. 1880).

R&R. Pool & Home, Inc. v. Zoning Board of Appeals, 43 Conn. App. 563, 684 A.2d 1207 (1996);

Haas Publ'g Co. v. Ind. Dep't of State Revenue, 835 *N.E.2d* 235 (2005).

In the Matter of Nancy Crawford-Hall, (No. B215368). An unpublished opinion of the California Court of Appeals, Lexis 3983, 38 Media L. Rep. 1975 (2010).

Other National and International Constitutions and Statutes of Law

2 *Eng. Stat. at Large* 191 (1341–1411).

Constitution of Kenya, 2010; see for example, sections 144, 148, 154, 155, 158, 167, 190, and Article 262, Transitional and Consequential Provisions, Commission for the Implementation of the Constitution.

Constitution of the Republic of Lithuania, 1992, Chapter 2, The Individual and the State.

European Union Council Directive, 27 June 1985, 85/377/EEC, Official Journal No. L175, 05/07/1985, p. 0040–0048.

General Provisions, Law on Provision of Information to the Public, Republic of Lithuania, No. 1–1418, July 2, 1996, as amended by No IX-2176, April 2004, Article 6 and Article 21.

Germany Constitution (2009), Articles 1–19, Article 42 (3).

Japan Bankruptcy Act of 2004, Act No. 75, June 2, 2004, amended in 2006 by Act No. 109.
Japan Bankruptcy Act of 2004, Article 26.
Japan Bankruptcy Act of 2004, Article 32.
Japan Bankruptcy Act of 2004, Article 136.
Japan Bankruptcy Act of 2004, Article 139.
Japan Bankruptcy Act of 2004, Article 197.
Japan Bankruptcy Act of 2004, Chapter IX, Article 216.
Lithuania Law on Provision of Information to the Public, Article 6 and Article 14(3), Right to Receive Information from State and Municipal Institutions and Agencies (2004).
Lithuania Law on Provision of Information to the Public Article 13 and Article 14, Protection of Individual Rights and Human Dignity, and Protection of Privacy, (2004).
Switzerland Constitution, Art. 17.
The Constitution of the Independent State of Samoa, as amended 2005, Election of the Head of State, First Schedule, Article 18.
The Political Constitution of the United Mexican States, as Amended to 2010, States of the Federation and the Federal District, Fifth Title, Article 115.
The Procurement Act of 2004, Sierra Leone, No. 14, Part IV, General Provisions on Procurement Proceedings, Section 26, Public notice of contract awards.
Treaty Between the United States and Senegal Concerning the Reciprocal Encourage and Protection of Investment, Article III, 1(e), 1983.
Treaty of Friendship, Commerce and Navigation between the U.S. and the Republic of Korea, Article XIV 3(a), 1956.

Other National and International Case Law

Court of Justice of the European Union (Fourth Chamber), Case C-279/11 heard June 1, 2011, and decided December 19, 2012, pp. 14–17 (#33–36) referencing Regulation 19(2).
Herbert v. Ashburner, 95 Eng. Rep. 628, Hilary Term, 24 Geo. II 297 (1750).
Rex v. Fraternity of Hostmen, 93 Eng. Rep. 1144 (1745).
Rex v. The Guardians, et al., 109 Eng. Rep. 202, 9 B. & C. 541, 542 (1829).

BIBLIOGRAPHY OF WEBSITES AND UNIVERSAL RESOURCE LOCATORS

Acts and Regulations Publication Act 1989, No. 142, Sections 18–35 (2007), http://www.legislation.govt.nz/act/public/1989/0142/latest/DLM195098.html, viewed March 2013.

Algeria, Public Notice of Telecommunication Regulations, http://www.arpt.dz/fr/pub/bult/, viewed June 4, 2013.

American Association of Law Libraries, State-By-State Report on Authentication of Online Legal Resources (2007), http://www.aallnet.org/aallwash/authen_rprt/authenfinalreport.pdf.

American Civil Liberties Union, "Protecting Civil Liberties in the Digital Age," http://www.aclu.org/protecting-civil-liberties-digital-age, viewed January 2013.

Argentina, http://www.scp.com.ar/doc/SituacionConcursal/SCP-Edicto_Asamblea_22–06–12.pdf, viewed June 19, 2013.

Argentina, Frio Industrias, http://www.frioindustrias.com.ar/actual/en/new.htm, viewed June 19, 2013.

Australian Government, government notice gazette, http://australia.gov.au/publications/australian-government-gazettes#GovernmentNoticesGazette, viewed June 13, 2013.

Australian Government, public consultations, http://australia.gov.au/news-and-media/public-consultations, viewed June 13, 2013.

Bank of Papua New Guinea, Public Notices, http://www.bankpng.gov.pg/exchange-control-mainmenu-138/public-notice, viewed June 13, 2013.

Belize Department of Environment, Environmental Compliance Plans, http://www.doe.gov.bz/ECP/ECPs/Belize ECPs/BZE 2004 ECPs/Belize Fifth Power Development Project 2004 ECPL.pdf.

Belize Department of Environment, Environmental Impact Assessment, http://www.doe.gov.bz/, all viewed June 13, 2013.

Belize Department of Environment, Environmental Impact Assessment, Report for Annex 20X, http://www.doe.gov.bz/documents/EIA/Chrysalis/Annex 20X–Public_Consultation_Report_for_Chrysalis Edited.pdf.

Bienvenue sur le site official de la ville d'Avion, http://www.ville-avion.fr/-Avis-public-.html, viewed June 12, 2013.

The Boston Globe, "Obama to Cabinet: Time for Belt-Tightening," http://www.boston.com/news/politics/politicalintelligence/2009/04/obama_to_cabine.html.

Brazil, "Mercosur launches public notices in December," http://www.brasil.gov.br/news/history/2012/11/12/mercosur-launches-public-notice-in-december-to-award-projects-to-eradicate-poverty-and-combat-hunger/newsitem_view?set_language=en, viewed June 19, 2013.

Brazil, Cultural Department, IV International Essay Competition, http://www.itamaraty.gov.br/temas/difusao-cultural/iv-concurso-internacional-de-monografias-lygia-fagundes-telles/iv-concurso-internacional-de-monografias-lygia-fagundes-telles-ing, viewed June 19, 2013.

Brazil, Elections, http://www.elections.gov.bz/modules/article_publish/files/files_4918ec65aafb8.pdf, p. 152, viewed June 13, 2013.

Brazil, Sacred Art Museum, http://www.museuartesacra.org.br/WYRPublicNotice.pdf, viewed June 19, 2013.

Central Bank of Nigeria, http://www.nairaland.com/64903/central-bank-nigeria-public-notice, viewed June 4, 2013.

CIA Factbook, https://www.cia.gov/library/publications/the-world-factbook/fields/2128.html, viewed June 3, 2013.

Coalition Provisional Authority, Iraq Central Bank, Development Fund, http://www.dod.mil/pubs/foi/operation_and_plans/CPA_ORHA/11_F_0117Doc94_Coalition_Provisional_Authority_Public_Notice_Regarding_Creation_of_Iraqi_Central_Bank_Development-Fund_forIraq.pdf, viewed June 5, 2013.

Courts Advertising, http://courtsad.blogspot.com/p/blog-page.html, viewed July 17, 2013.

Data security policy issues at the turn of the century, http://www.sans.org/reading_room/whitepapers/backup/electronic-data-retention-policy_514, viewed July 29, 2013.

Egypt, Information and Decision Support Center, Recent Publication, http://www.idsc.gov.eg/default.aspx, viewed June 5, 2013.

Egypt's IDSC Information Portal, http://www.eip.gov.eg/AboutEIP/AboutEIP.aspx, viewed June 5, 2013.

The Electoral Amendment Act 2002, New Zealand http://www.legislation.govt.nz/act/public/2002/0001/latest/DLM130605.html, viewed March 2013.

Electronic Frontier Foundation, https://www.eff.org/work, viewed January 2013.

Embassy of Algeria to the United States of America, http://www.algerianembassy.org/consular_affairs/moving.html, reviewed June 4, 2013.

Fact Sheet No. 1, The Legislative Process in Tanzania, Publication of Bills, http://www.parliament.go.tz/index.php/home/pages/15 (March 2013).

"Federal forfeiture notices will soon be on-line only," http://www.acfcs.org/federal-forfeiture-notices-will-soon-be-on-line-only/, viewed January 2013.

FOI Law Spreading Around the World, http://www.wri.org/stories/2010/09/freedom-information-laws-spreading-around-world, viewed January 2013.

France, public comment, http://www.pays-de-lure.fr/vivre_en_pays_de_lure/avis-public-insertion-1.pdf, viewed June 12, 2013.

Freedom of Information: The right to know, http://unesdoc.unesco.org/images/0019/001936/193653e.pdf, viewed January 2013.

GlobalTenders, http://www.globaltenders.com/global_tenders_FAQ.htm, viewed July 17, 2013.

GlobalTenders, http://www.globaltenders.com/index.htm, viewed July 17, 2013.

Guaymas, Port Services, http://www.puertodeguaymas.com.mx/news/46-home/193-the-port-of-guaymas-public-notice-to-those-interested-in-participating-in-the-process-of-opening-to-private-investment, viewed June 19, 2013.

Guidelines for Digital Newspaper Preservation Readiness, p. 3, http://publishing.educopia.org/chronicles/, viewed July 23, 2013.

History flushed, The Economist, April 28, 2012, http://www.economist.com/node/21553410, viewed July 29, 2013.

ICT, http://www.ictregulationtoolkit.org/en/Publication.3573.html, reviewed June 4, 2013.

Industrial Technology Research Institute, Hsinchu, Taiwan, Republic of China, "Guidelines on the Management and Implementation of Intellectual Property Rights," http://www.itri.org.tw/eng/econtent/copyright/copyright01.aspx, viewed June 24, 2013.

"Instructions for completing notice of elections to be exempt," http://pooplus.x10.mx/forms/FL-DWC-250-i.pdf, viewed June 19, 2013.

Internet Users in the Middle East, June 30, 2012, www.internetworldstats.com, viewed June 5, 2013.

Internet users, population and Facebook statistics for Africa, 2012, Internet World Stats, www.internetworldstats.com, viewed June 5, 2013.

Internet users, population and Facebook statistics for the Middle East, 2012, Internet World Stats, www.internetworldstats.com, viewed June 12, 2013.

Investor Guide, http://www.mofa.gov.iq/documentfiles/InvestorGuide.pdf, viewed June 5, 2013.

Iraqi Securities Commission, http://www.isc.gov.iq/sites/isc.gov.iq/files/SecuritiesLawEnglish-version.pdf, page 27, viewed June 5, 2013.

Israel Export & International Cooperation Institute, http://dgm.export.gov.il/, viewed July 22, 2013.

Israel State Archives, Declassified Archival Material, http://www.archives.gov.il/ArchiveGov_Eng/Our+Holdings/collection/, viewed July 22, 2013.

Israel State Archives, Notices for the Public, http://www.archives.gov.il/ArchiveGov_Eng/about/Notices2/, viewed July 22, 2013.

Israel, Airport Authority, http://www.iaa.gov.il/Rashat/en-US/Rashot/MessagesArchive/SpokesMan/msg151012.htm, viewed June 5, 2013.

Israel, Ministry of Health, http://www.health.gov.il/English/Services/MedicalAndHealthProfessions/OccupationalTherapist/Pages/Notice.aspx, viewed June 5, 2013.

Kingdom of Morocco Ministry of Justice and Freedom, Procedures in Family Justice, http://adala.justice.gov.ma/production/Guides_Manuels/fr/PlaquetteANG.pdf, viewed June 5, 2013.

Labeling Criteria, http://www.puntofocal.gov.ar/notific_otros_miembros/tpkm34_t.pdf, viewed June 19, 2013.

Letter from Susan M. Baer, director, Aviation Department of the Port Authority of New York and New Jersey, http://panynj.gov/airports/, viewed April 2013.

LG Chem, Material Safety Data Sheet, SBS (LG-411)Cas No. 9003–55–8, http://www.lgchem.com.tr/products/16122012–181558-msds_lg411_e.pdf, viewed June 12, 2013.

The Local Electoral Act of 2001, New Zealand, http://www.legislation.govt.nz/act/public/2001/0035/latest/DLM94309.html, viewed March 2013.

Margaret Hedstrom, Digital Preservation: Problems and Prospects, http://www.dl.slis.tsukuba.ac.jp/DLjournal/No_20/1-hedstrom/1-hedstrom.html.

Maroc Telecom, 2010 Registration Document, http://www.iam.ma/Lists/Tlchargement 20Finance/Attachments/345/MarocTelecom-Document-Reference-2010-VERSION-ANGLAISE.pdf, viewed June 4, 2013.

Melanesian Trustee Services Limited, Notices to Unit Holders, http://www.mtsl.com.pg/main/href/0c/news/.

METRO AG, Düsseldorf, Public notice of the additional cash payment for the benefit of the former outside shareholders of ASKO Deutsche Kaufhaus AG, http://www.metrogroup.de/internet/site/metrogroup/get/documents/metrogroup_international/corpsite/05_inrel/publications/disclosures-13–01–04-ASKO-en.pdf, viewed June 12, 2013.

Ministry of Business, Innovation and Employment, New Zealand, http://www.business.govt.nz/companies, viewed January 2013.

Monaco Public Services, "How to nominate someone for an honorary distinction," http://en.service-public-particuliers.gouv.mc/You-and-The-Administration/Honours/Honours/How-to-nominate-someone-for-an-honorary-distinction, viewed June 12, 2013.

Monaco Public Services Announcements, http://en.service-public-particuliers.gouv.mc/Announcements2/Stamps-to-go-on-sale-on-5-July-2013, viewed June 12, 2013.

Monaco Public Services for Business VAT Tax Invoices http://en.service-public-entreprises.gouv.mc/Tax/VAT/Statements/Invoices-Obligatory-notices, viewed July 22, 2013.

Monaco Public Services List of Paid Holidays 2013, http://en.service-public-particuliers.gouv.mc/Announcements2/List-of-paid-public-holidays-in-2013, viewed June 12, 2013.

Monaco Public Services, http://en.service-public-entreprises.gouv.mc/, viewed June 12, 2013.

Morocco, public service, http://www.service-public.ma/en/Web/guest/.

Morocco, Speech Addressed to the Nation by His Majesty King Mohammed VI, http://www.emergence.gov.ma/en/Pacte/Pages/LePacte.aspx, viewed June 5, 2013.

Move to Online Public Notices Looms Over Newspapers, http://usatoday30.usatoday.com/tech/news/2009–05–22-online-notices_N.htm, viewed July 22, 2013.

MyPublicNotice.com, http://www.mypublicnotices.com/PublicNotice.asp?Page=WhatArePublicNotices, viewed July 16, 2013.

National Ports Agency, http://www.anp.org.ma/En/Agency/Pages/Governance.aspx, viewed June 5, 2013.

NCTA Papua New Guinea Public Notices, http://mail.pangtel.gov.pg/Pages/Home.aspx, viewed June 13, 2013.

Nesbiye Aydin Schools, http://www.nesibeaydin.k12.tr/okul/index.php?option=com_content&view=article&id=447:emniyet-genel-mueduerluegue-kamu-spotu&catid=94&Itemid=511&lang=en, viewed June 12, 2013.

Netanya Municipality, http://www.netanya.muni.il/Eng/?CategoryID=1598&ArticleID=2144, viewed June 5, 2013.

New Study Quantifies Use of Social Media in Arab Spring, http://www.washington.edu/news/2011/09/12/new-study-quantifies-use-of-social-media-in-arab-spring/, viewed June 5, 2013.

New Zealand Department of Internal Affairs, Gazette, http://www.dia.govt.nz/Services-New-Zealand-Gazette-Index, viewed June 13, 2013.

New Zealand Department of Internal Affairs, Legal Policies, http://www.dia.govt.nz/diawebsite.nsf/wpg_URL/Services-New-Zealand-Gazette-Legal-Policies Open Document, viewed July 18, 2013.

New Zealand Department of Internal Affairs, Statistics, http://www.dia.govt.nz/Data-and-statistics, viewed July 18, 2013.

New Zealand Government, statistics, https://data.govt.nz/latest-data-requests/, viewed July 18, 2013.

Nice, Open Access, http://www.nice.fr/Media/Files/Avis-public-POS, viewed June 12, 2013.

Nigerian Copyright Commission, http://www.copyright.gov.ng/index.php/public-notice, viewed June 4, 2013.

Nigerian Electricity Regulatory Commission, http://www.nercng.org/index.php/media-and-publicity/public-notices, viewed June 4, 2013.

Ningbo, China, Public Notice of Appliance Wiring Material UL Style 3321, http://www.finanznachrichten.de/nachrichten-2013–04/26489102-public-notice-on-potentially-hazardous-appliance-wiring-008.htm, viewed June 12, 2013.

Ningbo, China, UL Style 3321, Hazard, http://www.prnewswire.com/news-releases/public-notice-on-potentially-hazardous-appliance-wiring-202314351.html.

Notice&Comment.com, http://www.noticeandcomment.com/about-us.aspx, http://www.noticeandcomment.com/how-to-use-this-site.aspx, http://www.noticeandcomment.com/search-press-releases.aspx, viewed June 4, 2013.

Office of the Administrator of the Coalition Provisional Authority, Baghdad, Iraq, http://dosfan.lib.uic.edu/ERC/cpa/english/regulations/PN1.pdf, viewed June 5, 2013.

Overview of all FOI law around the world, 2011 update, http://www.llrx.com/features/foilawsoverview.htm, viewed January 2013.

Papua New Guinea, Department of Lands and Physical Planning, http://www.lands.gov.pg/Public_Notice/Secretary.html, viewed June 13, 2013.

Papua New Guinea, University of Technology, public notice announcements, http://www.unitech.ac.pg/index.php?option=com_content&view=article&id=74:public-notice&-catid=169:news-public-notices&Itemid=89; viewed June 12, 2013.

Peru, National Institute for the Defense of Competition and Protection of Intellectual Property, Chapter 8, Trade Remedies, http://www.indecopi.gob.pe/repositorioaps/0/5/jer/legislation_ve/Trade_Remedies_US.pdf, viewed June 19, 2013.

PNG Ports, http://www.pngports.com.pg/docs/Public-notices/PNGPCL_CCD1011_PUBLIC-NOTICE-Queens-Birthday.pdf, viewed June 13, 2013.

Post Courier, Papua New Guinea, http://www.postcourier.com.pg/20120502/news01.htm, viewed June 12, 2013.

Public Notice Board, http://i-uv.com/post-your-courtesy-notices-for-the-world-community-to-acknowledge/, viewed July 17, 2013.

Public Notice for VSAT operators at http://www.cmc.iq/en/pdfcmc/CMC VSAT public notice.pdf, "Public Notice on the Period for Handling Filings for Approval of Concerted Action by Enterprises," http://www.apeccp.org.tw/doc/Taipei/Decision/ctdec037.htm, http://english.taipei.gov.tw/ct.asp?xItem=1803812&ctNode=32871&mp=100002.

PublicNotice.org, http://thepublicnotice.org/about/, viewed May 28, 2013, http://thepublicnotice.org/about/faq/; http://thepublicnotice.org/about/staff/; http://thepublicnotice.org/terms-of-use/; all viewed May 28, 2013.

Public notices, http://www.islamicsolutions.com/about/public-notice/, viewed January 2013.

Public notices, http://www.ul.com/global/por/pages/corporate/newsroom/publicnotices/, viewed January 2013.

Public Policy and Funding the News: Insult to Injury, http://fundingthenews.usc.edu/related_research/6_Carnegie_PublicNotice.pdf, viewed July 22, 2013.

SGS Peru, Pre-Shipment Inspection – Angola – Logistics, http://www.sgs.pe/en/Logistics/Transportation/Containers/Pre-Shipment-Inspection-PSI/Pre-Shipment-Inspection-Angola.aspx, viewed June 19, 2013.

Shannon E. Martin, Snapshot summary data for public notice laws in each state of the U.S., http://watchnotice.wordpress.com/research/2011–2/, viewed February 2013.

Shannon E. Martin, State-Level Legislative and Court Activity 2006–2007, http://watchnotice.wordpress.com/research/2007–2/, viewed February 2013.

Singapore National Library, Newspaper Pages, http://newspapers.nl.sg/Digitised/Article/straitstimes19160524–1.2.47.aspx, viewed June 24, 2013.

Surfing and Site Guide, About Us, http://www.internetworldstats.com/surfing.htm, viewed June 12, 2013.

Suzanna Conrad, Key Issues, Prairienet, http://www.prairienet.org/op/digarch/key-issues/.

Times of India, "Deputy directors to conduct beach inspections," http://articles.timesofindia.indiatimes.com/2013–06–09/goa/39849159_1_shacks-tourism-department-tourism-season.

Turkey, Ministry of Foreign Affairs, http://www.mfa.gov.tr/chapter-i_-conditions-of-residence-and-business.en.mfa, viewed June 12, 2013.

Turkish Academy of Science, http://akademi.tuba.gov.tr/en/haberler/tuba-dan-haberler/kurum-dan-haberler/1580-tuerkye-blmler-akadems-kamuoyu-bldrs.html, viewed June 12, 2013.

U.S. Department of Justice Forfeiture Listings, http://www.forfeiture.gov/, viewed July 22, 2013.

Vannevar Bush, As We May Think, *The Atlantic*, July 1, 1945, http://www.theatlantic.com/magazine/archive/1945/07/as-we-may-think/303881/, viewed July 29, 2013.

The Washington Post, "Trimming the Federal Fat, Part One," http://voices.washingtonpost.com/federal-eye/2009/04/trimming_the_federal_fat_part.html; all viewed July 22, 2013.

World Trade Organization, Committee on Technical Barriers to Trade, August 20, 2010, http://www.puntofocal.gov.ar/doc/2a104belice.pdf, viewed June 13, 2013.

Zhong Lun Law Firm Newsletter, "China Legal Update, Tax Treaty," August 2012, http://www.ilntoday.com/files/2012/08/ZL-Newsletter_201208.pdf, viewed June 24, 2013.

INDEX

A

B

M

N

O

P

W

X

Y